Luke

The Story of Salvation Fulfilled

JEFF CAVINS and JEFFREY MORROW

West Chester, Pennsylvania

Luke: The Story of Salvation Fulfilled has been submitted for ecclesiastical review and *imprimatur* to the Archdiocese of Philadelphia.

© 2024 Ascension Publishing Group, LLC. All rights reserved.

With the exception of short excerpts used in articles and critical reviews, no part of this work may be reproduced, transmitted, or stored in any form whatsoever, printed or electronic, without the prior written permission of the publisher.

Unless otherwise noted, Scripture passages are from the Revised Standard Version–Second Catholic Edition (Ignatius Edition) © 2006 National Council of the Churches of Christ in the United States of America. Used by permission. All rights reserved.

The Scripture text marked "NAB" is from the New American Bible © 1970 Confraternity of Christian Doctrine, Washington, DC, and is used by permission. All rights reserved.

Excerpts from the English translation of the *Catechism of the Catholic Church* for use in the United States of America © 1994 United States Catholic Conference, Inc.–Libreria Editrice Vaticana. Used by permission. English translation of the *Catechism of the Catholic Church: Modifications from the Editio Typica* © 1997 United States Conference of Catholic Bishops–Libreria Editrice Vaticana.

Ascension
PO Box 1990
West Chester, PA 19380
1-800-376-0520
ascensionpress.com

Cover design: Faceout Studio, Sarah Stueve

Printed in the United States of America

ISBN: 979-8-89276-023-2

CONTENTS

About *Luke: The Story of Salvation Fulfilled* v

Getting the Most Out of This Study xvi

Session One: Introduction to Luke 1

Session Two: Luke 1–3, The Early Life of Jesus 11

Session Three: Luke 4–6, Jesus Begins His Public Ministry 27

Session Four: Luke 7–9, The Mission and Miracles of Jesus 39

Session Five: Luke 10–12, Sharing in Jesus' Mission 55

Session Six: Luke 13–17, Following Jesus 69

Session Seven: Luke 18–21, The Triumphal Entry
and the End Times 83

Session Eight: Luke 22–24, The Death,
Resurrection, and Ascension of Jesus 95

Responses to the Discussion Questions 109

Notes 144

For Further Reading 145

About the Authors and Presenters 146

Program Credits 147

ABOUT *LUKE: THE STORY OF SALVATION FULFILLED*

Luke: The Story of Salvation Fulfilled explores the life and teachings of Jesus Christ as told by St. Luke the Evangelist. Beginning with the foretelling of John the Baptist's birth and continuing through Jesus' public ministry, passion, death, Resurrection, and ascension, Luke's narrative shows us how Jesus fulfills the Old Testament prophesies and everything that Scripture foretold about the promised Messiah. As you journey through Luke's account, you will encounter Jesus in a new way and discover how his teachings fit into your life today.

MATERIALS
What do I need for this study?

Materials for *Luke: The Story of Salvation Fulfilled* include the following:

- **Workbook:** This contains session summaries, the daily reading plan, questions for reflection and discussion, video outlines, responses to the questions, and supplementary information relevant to Luke and his Gospel account. *You will need one workbook for every participant, study leader, and small group facilitator.*

- **Video Presentations**: These video presentations by Jeff Cavins and Dr. Jeffrey Morrow provide comprehensive teaching and commentary on Luke's Gospel. They are available online or for purchase as a DVD set.

In addition to the workbook and video presentations, every participant and facilitator should have a copy of a Catholic Bible and the *Catechism of the Catholic Church*. For this study, we recommend **The Great Adventure Catholic Bible**, which incorporates the color-coded *Bible Timeline*® Learning System along with informative side features and helpful contextual information throughout. We also recommend the **Ascension edition of the *Catechism***, which uses the color-coded **Foundations of Faith** approach. Both are available at Ascensionpress.com.

> *Note:* You can access both *The Great Adventure Catholic Bible* and the *Catechism of the Catholic Church*, Ascension Edition, without charge through the Ascension App, available at Ascensionpress.com/app.

< *Saint Luke* by Giorgio Vasari

LENGTH
How long will it take to complete this study, start to finish?
How much time will I need to spend on each session at home?

Number of Sessions

Luke: The Story of Salvation Fulfilled has eight sessions: the Introduction session and seven content sessions. Groups that meet weekly and follow the daily reading plan can finish the entire study in fifty days.

Individual Investment

The assigned reading and questions vary from session to session. We recommend allowing yourself about fifteen minutes a day to complete each day's assigned chapters in Luke and respond to the corresponding questions.

LUKE: THE STORY OF SALVATION FULFILLED DAILY READING PLAN

Day	Study Reading	Topics
	Session One: Introduction	
1	Session One Meeting Day	
	Session Two: Luke 1–3	
2	Luke 1:1–38	Dedication to Theophilus The Birth of John the Baptist Foretold The Birth of Jesus Foretold
3	Luke 1:39–80	Mary Visits Elizabeth; and Mary's Song of Praise The Birth of John the Baptist Zechariah's Prophecy
4	Luke 2:1–21	The Birth of Jesus The Shepherds and the Angels Jesus Is Circumcised and Named
5	Luke 2:22–52	Jesus Is Presented in the Temple The Return to Nazareth The Boy Jesus in the Temple
6	Luke 3:1–20	The Preaching of John the Baptist
7	Luke 3:21–38	The Baptism of Jesus The Ancestry of Jesus
8	Session Two Meeting Day	

LUKE DAILY READING PLAN (cont.)

Day	Study Reading	Topics
		Session Three: Luke 4–6
9	Luke 4:1–30	The Temptation of Jesus Jesus Begins Preaching and Teaching in Galilee The Rejection of Jesus at Nazareth
10	Luke 4:31–44	The Man with an Unclean Spirit Healings at Simon's House Jesus Preaches in the Synagogues of Judea
11	Luke 5:1–16	Jesus Calls the First Disciples Jesus Cleanses a Leper
12	Luke 5:17–39	Jesus Heals a Paralytic Jesus Calls Levi The Question About Fasting
13	Luke 6:1–26	A Teaching About the Sabbath The Man with a Withered Hand Jesus Chooses the Twelve Disciples Jesus Teaches and Heals Blessings and Woes
14	Luke 6:27–49	Love for Enemies Judging Others A Tree and Its Fruit Hearers and Doers
15	Session Three Meeting Day	
		Session Four: Luke 7–9
16	Luke 7:1–17	Jesus Heals a Centurion's Slave Jesus Raises a Widow's Son at Nain
17	Luke 7:18–50	Messengers from John the Baptist A Sinful Woman Forgiven
18	Luke 8:1–25	Some Women Accompany Jesus The Parable of the Sower The Explanation of the Parable A Lamp Is Not Hidden The True Kindred of Jesus Jesus Calms a Storm on the Sea
19	Luke 8:26–56	Jesus Heals the Gerasene Demoniac A Girl Restored to Life and a Woman Healed
20	Luke 9:1–27	The Mission of the Twelve Herod's Perplexity Feeding the Five Thousand Peter's Declaration That Jesus Is the Christ Taking Up One's Cross

LUKE DAILY READING PLAN (cont.)

Day	Study Reading	Topics
		Session Four: Luke 7–9 (cont.)
21	Luke 9:28–62	The Transfiguration Jesus Heals a Boy with a Demon Jesus Again Foretells his Death True Greatness Another Exorcist A Samaritan Village Refuses to Receive Jesus Would-Be Followers of Jesus
22	Session Four Meeting Day	
		Session Five: Luke 10–12
23	Luke 10:1–24	The Mission of the Seventy Woes to Unrepentant Cities The Return of the Seventy Jesus Rejoices and Thanks the Father
24	Luke 10:25–42	The Parable of the Good Samaritan Jesus Visits Martha and Mary
25	Luke 11:1–26	The Lord's Prayer Perseverance in Prayer Jesus and Be-elzebul The Return of the Unclean Spirit
26	Luke 11:27–54	True Blessedness The Sign of Jonah The Light of the Body Jesus Denounces the Hypocrisy of the Pharisees and Lawyers
27	Luke 12:1–34	A Warning Against Hypocrisy Whom to Fear The Parable of the Rich Fool Do Not Be Anxious
28	Luke 12:35–59	The Necessity of Watchfulness The Faithful and the Unfaithful Servant Jesus the Cause of Division Interpreting the Present Time Settling with Your Accuser
29	Session Five Meeting Day	

LUKE DAILY READING PLAN (cont.)

Day	Study Reading	Topics
	**Session Six: Luke 13–17**	
30	Luke 13:1–17	Repent or Perish The Parable of the Barren Fig Tree Jesus Heals a Crippled Woman
31	Luke 13:18–35	The Parable of the Mustard Seed The Parable of the Leaven The Narrow Door The Lament over Jerusalem
32	Luke 14:1–35	Jesus Heals the Man with Dropsy on the Sabbath Humility and Hospitality The Parable of the Great Banquet The Cost of Discipleship About Salt
33	Luke 15:1–32	The Parable of the Lost Sheep The Parable of the Lost Coin The Parable of the Prodigal and His Brother
34	Luke 16:1–31	The Parable of the Dishonest Steward The Law and the Kingdom of God The Rich Man and Lazarus
35	Luke 17:1–37	Some Sayings of Jesus Jesus Cleanses Ten Lepers The Coming of the Kingdom
36	Session Six Meeting Day	
	**Session Seven: Luke 18–21**	
37	Luke 18:1–43	The Parable of the Widow and the Unrighteous Judge The Parable of the Pharisees and the Tax Collector Jesus Blesses the Children The Rich Ruler A Third Time Jesus Foretells His Death and Resurrection Jesus Heals a Blind Beggar near Jericho
38	Luke 19:1–27	Jesus and Zacchaeus The Parable of the Ten Pounds
39	Luke 19:28–48	Jesus' Entry into Jerusalem Jesus Weeps over Jerusalem Jesus Cleanses the Temple
40	Luke 20:1–18	The Authority of Jesus Questioned The Parable of the Wicked Tenants
41	Luke 20:19–47	The Question About Paying Taxes The Question About Man's Resurrection A Question About the Messiah Jesus Denounces the Hypocrisy of the Scribes

LUKE DAILY READING PLAN (cont.)

Day	Study Reading	Topics
	**Session Seven: Luke 18–21 (cont.)**	
42	Luke 21:1–38	The Widow's Offering The Destruction of the Temple Foretold Signs and Persecutions The Destruction of Jerusalem Foretold The Coming of the Son of Man The Lesson of the Fig Tree Exhortation to Watchfulness
43	Session Seven Meeting Day	
	**Session Eight: Luke 22–24**	
44	Luke 22:1–34	The Conspiracy to Kill Jesus The Preparation of the Passover Jesus Institutes the Eucharist The Dispute About Greatness Peter's Denial Foretold
45	Luke 22:35–71	Purse, Bag, and Sword Jesus Prays on the Mount of Olives The Betrayal and Arrest of Jesus Peter Denies Jesus The Mocking and Beating of Jesus Jesus Before the Council
46	Luke 23:1–25	Jesus Before Pilate Jesus Before Herod Jesus Sentenced to Death
47	Luke 23:26–56	The Crucifixion of Jesus The Death of Jesus The Burial of Jesus
48	Luke 24:1–35	The Resurrection of Jesus The Walk to Emmaus
49	Luke 24:36–53	Jesus Appears to His Disciples The Ascension of Jesus
50	Session Eight Meeting Day	

STRUCTURE
How are the study sessions organized?
What are the main components of each session?

Each session is broken into two parts: **home preparation** and **small group meeting**.

HOME PREPARATION: Overview, Read, Respond

Each session begins with personal study at home that involves reviewing the context of the session, reading the Scripture selections, and responding to questions that will help you think more deeply about what you have read.

Overview

The overview helps you enter Luke's Gospel by introducing the key figures, events, and themes in the session's assigned chapters. It provides context for what you are about to read in Scripture. We recommend reading the overview on the first day of each session of the week.

Read and Respond

The assignments for each session are outlined in the daily reading plan, which conveniently breaks up the Gospel of Luke into reading selections and questions that you can complete between small group meetings. We recommend that you allow yourself *at least fifteen minutes* to complete each day's assigned reading and question.

> *Helpful Tip:* Reading the Gospel and answering the questions may bring further questions to mind. When they do, write down your thoughts and questions so that you can bring them up during your small group discussion. It is also a good idea to take note of the names, locations, and events described in the Scripture reading that stand out for you.

As you write your responses to the questions, *we strongly recommend that you refrain from checking the responses* in the back of the workbook until *after* you meet and discuss the questions with your small group.

Application

The final step of the home preparation for each session involves applying the lessons from Luke's Gospel to your own life by taking a few minutes for reflection, commitment, and prayer. We recommend doing the application step on the last day of home preparation for each session to prepare for your small group meeting.

SMALL GROUP MEETING: Discuss, Watch, Review

Meeting in a small group to discuss the study questions is a time for fellowship and for sharing questions and insights. As a group, you will begin by *discussing* your responses to the questions, *watching* the video presentation, and *reviewing* what you have learned. Your group may also decide to review the responses in the back of the workbook together, or you can read them later at home.

As you participate in your small group meeting, it is very important that you and your group follow the ten commandments for small group discussion:

Ten Commandments for Small Group Discussion

1. Enjoy yourself!
2. Speak with respect and charity.
3. Do not ridicule or dismiss what others say. Keep comments positive.
4. Come prepared.
5. If you were not able to prepare, let others speak first.
6. Stick to the topic and questions at hand.
7. Start and end on time.
8. Allow silence. Give people a chance to think.
9. Listen to others without interrupting.
10. Keep personal matters within the group.

—Adapted from Thomas Smith's original "10 Commandments of a Small Group"

Each small group is different. Therefore, how you choose to conduct these small group gatherings—from the length of each meeting to how you approach the discussion and video presentation—depends on the needs of each group. For the best experience during your meeting, we recommend completing these steps in the following order:

Discuss

In this conversation, members of your group will have an opportunity to share insights, reflections, and further questions about the readings and discussion questions. The goal of the discussion is for the group to engage in fellowship and share ideas for applying Luke's Gospel to everyday life. Trained facilitators should guide the small group discussion and keep it on track.

Watch

After the discussion, the video presentation provides a deeper reflection on Luke's Gospel, its historical and cultural context, and its larger influence on the Church today, especially in relation to the celebration of the Eucharist. It provides a richer understanding of Luke's Gospel, with a special emphasis on ways to apply what you have learned to your life.

> *Video Outline:* The workbook includes an outline for each video, highlighting the main points of the presentation. As you watch, use the space provided to write down the connections you notice, the questions that arise, and whatever else stands out for you.

Review

Following the video presentation (and depending on time), your group may decide to reflect more deeply on what you have learned in this session by discussing the video or by looking through the responses to the discussion questions in the back of the workbook. However you choose to continue the conversation or conclude your time together, this final reflective stage of the meeting should serve as both a wrap-up for the present session and a launching point for the upcoming home preparation.

A Note About Workbook Responses

The first purpose of the responses provided in the back of the workbook is to help participants review this week's session and establish the context for the next session. Therefore, the best time to read the responses is when you start the home preparation for the next session. The second purpose of the responses is to provide helpful insights for small group facilitators as they lead group discussions. Facilitators should also complete the Scripture reading and answer the questions on their own before reading the responses.

FORMAT
What's the general sequence for small group meetings?

Starting Off: Session One

Session One is essentially your kickoff meeting for this study. Your goals for the first session are to ensure that everyone feels welcome, has the study materials, and knows how the study works.

Session One does not require any home preparation or advance reading; for that reason, it is shorter than the other sessions in the study. This gives the people in your group time to get to know one another. Consider offering refreshments and other community-building activities. Also, we highly encourage your group to go over the "Ten Commandments for Small Group Discussion" (p. xii) so that everyone understands how best to engage and respect one another in discussion.

Session One may look something like this:

1. Welcome and group introductions (about 15 min)
2. Overview of the study (10 min)
3. Discussion (10 min)
4. Introduction video (30 min)
5. Reflections and fellowship time (15 min)

Gaining Momentum: Sessions Two through Eight

The remaining sessions of *Luke: The Story of Salvation Fulfilled* will lead you on a journey through Luke's Gospel and the fulfillment of God's Old Testament promises. Here is an example of what the remaining small group meetings could look like:

1. Welcome and intro (about 10 min)
2. Small group discussion (40 min)
3. Video presentation (30 min)
4. Closing review and prayer (about 10 min)

For more information about how to plan and promote a Bible study and how to facilitate a small group discussion, visit Ascensionpress.com or call 1-800-376-0520.

GETTING THE MOST OUT OF THIS STUDY

Here are some ways to make sure the time, effort, and energy you put into this study are worthwhile and will have a long-lasting impact.

Bring It to Prayer

Whenever you open your Bible to read, *start with prayer* and place yourself in God's presence. As you read, adopt an attitude of listening. Try to treat Scripture not as a text but as a personal message from God. What is he saying? What does it mean? What does it mean for your life? If you come to the Word focused on having an encounter with the Lord, he will speak to your heart, and you will be transformed.

Take the Time

God's Word is worthy of our time. Give yourself sufficient time to read and respond each day between your small group meetings. Build a habit of dwelling with God in his Word and discovering his personal message to you, delivered through the Scripture.

It may be tempting to save time by skipping personal reflection and simply looking at the responses provided in the workbook. However, these responses do not exhaust the meaning that can be found in the reading of Scripture. Reading a response written by someone else may satisfy your mind for a moment—but it will not result in the kind of growth you will experience if you attempt to answer the question on your own first. Likewise, a group of participants who have spent time pondering the Scripture passages will have more varied insights to discuss, which will lead to a more meaningful discussion.

Focus on Good Discussion

The success of a small group depends on a good discussion. A Bible study is not about simply watching a video presentation or reading commentary. The people in your group will have unique insights; the questions you ask and connections you make together will deepen your understanding and appreciation of Scripture in a way a simple lecture or self-study cannot.

Some individuals in your group may be naturally eager to speak up, while others are more inclined to wait and listen. It is in everyone's interest to help make sure each person in the group has a fair chance to share their thoughts. Follow the "Ten Commandments for Small Group Discussion" (p. xii) and be mindful of how you are contributing to the conversation. If you realize you have been speaking frequently while others have yet to express their own insights, consider pausing and inviting others to speak before you.

When you come to Scripture and your small group with the right mindset, you will have the opportunity to explore and receive the Word of God in ways you have yet to encounter. Follow these steps over time, and you will be more than fed: you will learn to feed yourself.

SESSION ONE

Introduction

OVERVIEW

Introduction to the Gospel of Luke

The Gospel according to Luke is one of the four accounts of the life of Jesus Christ contained in the New Testament. In fact, Luke the Evangelist authored *two* books in the New Testament: his Gospel and the Acts of the Apostles. They are essentially two parts of one longer narrative. Part one, Luke's Gospel, recounts the life, death, and Resurrection of Jesus and his fulfillment of Old Testament promises; part two, Acts, recounts the life of the early Church. In this study, Luke invites us to enter the story of Jesus Christ and make it our own.

Historical studies of the Gospels have shown that they were modeled on ancient Greek and Roman biographies—which means, among other things, that the Gospel authors were interested in getting the history right. The Gospels, however, are more than histories or biographies; they present an invitation to follow Jesus and have an intimate relationship with God. The earliest testimonies of Christian communal worship from the second century AD record that the Gospels were read each time Christians gathered to celebrate the Eucharist.[1] The Gospels prepared the baptized to receive the Eucharist, and there is evidence that the Gospel authors intended their accounts of Jesus' life to be read at Mass to help the baptized grow in the Faith.

Each of the four Gospels views the life and ministry of Jesus from a unique vantage point. Among them, the Gospel of Luke is unique in many respects. Tradition tells us that Luke was St. Paul's physician and traveling companion; this is supported indirectly by the internal evidence of the Gospel itself. There are many descriptions of healings and physical miracles that employ Greek terms that a physician might use; there are also similarities between Luke's Gospel and Paul's letters, like 1 Corinthians.

Although some scholars date the Gospel of Luke to as late as the eighties AD, Luke probably wrote his Gospel sometime before AD 62 since the sequel, Acts, makes no mention of the destruction of the Temple in Jerusalem (which occurred in AD 70), the martyrdoms of Peter and Paul (in the middle of the sixties AD), or the martyrdom of James, the early Church leader in Jerusalem, who was killed in AD 62. These omissions would be inexplicable if Acts, written after Luke's Gospel, was written after these events, since the destruction of the Temple was such an

Basilica of the Annunciation, Nazareth

important example of Jesus' prophetic fulfillment, and Peter, Paul, and James were such central figures in Acts.

Luke addressed his Gospel to one named "Theophilus." It is not clear who Theophilus is—perhaps a prominent early Christian, perhaps a Jewish high priest (a Theophilus served as high priest during the time of the apostle Paul), or perhaps a stand-in name for any given Christian (*Theophilus* means "lover of God"). The explicit reason Luke wrote his Gospel was to compile for Theophilus "a narrative of the things which have been accomplished among us" (Luke 1:1), providing an orderly account of the life of Jesus. It seems likely that what he was actually trying to do was to present the biography of Jesus in such a way that it fulfilled at least three purposes: (1) to provide a historical account in light of the other eyewitness testimony to Jesus' life that Luke investigated; (2) to highlight how Jesus' life brought the Old Testament to fulfillment as Jesus relived the history of Israel as a faithful Son of God; and (3) to be used in the liturgy to help the faithful understand and prepare for the fruitful reception of the sacraments.

One way into Luke's narrative is to picture yourself as one of the characters hidden in the crowds observing the events firsthand. In this way, you will come to know the life of Jesus more personally, and you will start to recognize your own life in the narratives of Scripture.

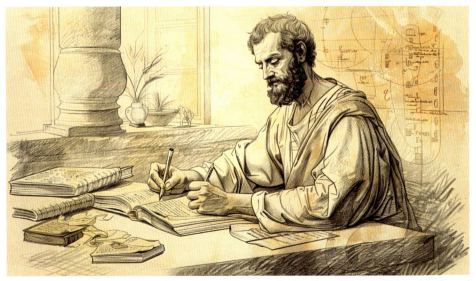

Illustrastion of St. Luke Writing His Gospel

SMALL GROUP MEETING - Day 1

Note: There is no home preparation for Session One.

DISCUSS

Before you begin reading Luke's Gospel, use the following discussion questions to share your thoughts and expectations with your group.

- *When we read the Gospels, we hope to learn more about Jesus, the one whom we should love above all others. In what ways has Jesus touched your life?*
- *What do you already know about the Gospel of Luke? What do you hope to learn from your study of Luke's Gospel?*

WATCH

 Session One: Introduction

Write down your notes and reflections on the video in the space provided.

I. **Introduction to the Gospel of Luke**

   A. Author of Gospel of Luke and Acts of the Apostles

   B. Emmaus road narrative

      1. Jesus reveals himself in two ways

         a. The Word of God (Liturgy of the Word)

         b. The Breaking of the Bread (Liturgy of the Eucharist)

      2. "The greatest Bible study in the history of the world"

II. **The Purpose of Luke's Gospel**

   A. Beginning of the Gospel

      1. Two disciples: Theophilus and the author (Luke)

2. Opening lines: narrative of the things that had to be fulfilled (Luke 1:1–4)

B. End of the Gospel

1. Two disciples: Cleopas and an unknown disciple (possibly Luke)

2. The Emmaus road narrative: Jesus begins with Moses and the prophets and shares all the things concerning himself (see Luke 24:27)

C. Proper response to the Gospel: obedience of faith

1. Intellectual assent

2. Personal entrusting of yourself to what you believe

III. **How This Study Works**

A. Bible reading and study

B. The small group experience

IV. **The Jewish Context of the Gospel of Luke**

A. Passover context with Jesus' teaching on the Eucharist

B. Luke's historical account: interviewed eyewitnesses

V. **St. Luke the Evangelist**

A. Who is the author? Luke, saint, Paul's traveling companion, physician

B. Theophilus ("lover of God"): high priest during St. Paul's lifetime (Josephus)

C. Greco-Roman biography: genre of ancient literature (including Gospels)

D. Mystagogy: how external signs signify spiritual realities

E. Senses of Scripture

1. Literal: "the meaning conveyed by the words of Scripture" (CCC 116)

2. Spiritual: the text of Scripture and how the realities and events within can be signs (CCC 117)

   a. Typological (allegorical): how Jesus prefigures the Church and the sacraments

   b. Topological (moral): how Scripture applies to the moral life

   c. Anagogical: how Scripture relates to eternal realities

VI. Conclusion

REVIEW

In his letter to the Colossians, Paul calls Luke "the beloved physician" (Colossians 4:14). Luke was a physician by trade, but he was also worthy of the title "beloved," which must refer to the way he lived Christian charity in his work. This "beloved physician," with his eye for detail, left us one of the four inspired biographies of Jesus. As you read through the Gospel of Luke at home, pay careful attention to the details that Luke provides.

CLOSING PRAYER

*Heavenly Father, thank you for giving your Church
four inspired accounts of the life of Jesus Christ.
Help us to grow in our relationship with you
through this study so that we can emulate Jesus
in our daily lives. Amen.*

FOR FURTHER STUDY

St. Luke the Author

St. Luke the Evangelist is best known as the author of the Gospel of Luke and its sequel, the Acts of the Apostles. Although he was not one of the twelve apostles, he was well positioned to write the Gospel of Luke and Acts because he was one of St. Paul's traveling companions; tradition also tells us that he served as St. Paul's physician. We can see from the narrative of Acts that there are many "we" passages in which Luke writes of Paul's travels in the first-person plural, "we" indicating that he was present there with Paul.

Kykkos Monastery, Cyprus. Mosaic. St. Luke, patron saint of icon painters.

The Greek of Luke's Gospel and of Acts is among the highest-quality writings of the New Testament, indicating that the author was very well educated. His Gospel includes many accounts of physical healings and the sort of details one might expect from a physician. A tradition also holds that Luke was an artist and painted the earliest depiction of the Blessed Virgin Mary. In light of these traditions, St. Luke is the patron saint of both artists and physicians.

See page 140 to view the icons attributed to St. Luke.

Jewish Luke?

Modern scholars commonly assume Luke was a Gentile, perhaps the only Gentile author of the New Testament. This is in part because, in Colossians, when Paul mentions "the only men of the circumcision among my fellow workers" (Colossians 4:11), Luke is not among them but appears only later (Colossians 4:14) as a fellow worker. In addition, the Greek of Luke's Gospel is very advanced compared with that of most of the other books of the New Testament.

There are subtle clues, however, that Luke might actually be Jewish, and possibly even a Jewish priest. How can this be, and how does it fit the tradition that Luke was a physician?

Regarding Paul's comments in Colossians, it is possible that "of the circumcision" may not be a reference to those who are Jewish but instead to a group of Jewish Christians who were mostly in conflict with Paul; it is also possible that among them, those who were named were the only members of that group who were his fellow workers. Moreover, "Luke" (*Loukas* in Greek) is a diminutive form of "Lucius" (*Loukios* in Greek). Thus, Luke may be the Lucius of Romans 16:21, whom Paul explicitly mentions as among his "fellow workers," which is Origen's view.[2] This may be the same Lucius of Cyrene (see Acts 13:1) in Antioch, which is where many early Christians believed Luke was from.

There are other indications of Luke's Jewish, possibly priestly, identity. Luke shows a very detailed knowledge of the Old Testament, often making subtle allusions. He focuses on the Temple and priesthood more than the other Gospels. If he were a Hellenistic Jew (many of the Jewish priests and Sadducees were Hellenized), it could explain his high level of Greek in comparison with that of the other New Testament writers. Moreover, Theophilus, to whom Luke addresses his narrative, may have been a high priest, indicated by the fact he is addressed as "most excellent" (Luke 1:3). In addition, there was a Theophilus, the son of Annas, who served as high priest from AD 37 to 41. In Acts, Luke mentions that Jewish priests have begun to follow Jesus (Acts 6:7).

◆ ❖ ◆

St. Jerome on Luke

At the end of the fourth century AD, St. Jerome wrote a short work titled *On Illustrious Men,* in which he described some of the earliest Christian saints. He included a brief description of Luke:

> Luke a physician of Antioch, as his writings indicate, was not unskilled in the Greek language. An adherent of the apostle Paul, and companion of all his journeying, he wrote a Gospel, concerning which the same Paul says, "We send with him a brother whose praise in the gospel is among all the churches," and to the Colossians, "Luke the beloved physician salutes you," and to Timothy, "Luke only is with me." He also wrote another excellent volume to which he prefixed the title *Acts of the Apostles,* a history which extends to the second year of Paul's sojourn at Rome, that is to the fourth year of Nero, from which we learn that the book was composed in that same city. … Some suppose that whenever Paul in his epistle says "according to my gospel," he means the book of Luke and that Luke not only was taught the gospel history by the apostle Paul who was not with the Lord in the flesh, but also by other apostles. This he too at the beginning of his work declares, saying "Even as they delivered unto us, which from the beginning were eyewitnesses and ministers of the word." So he wrote the gospel as he had heard it, but composed the Acts of the Apostles as he himself had seen.[3]

Statue of Saint Luke the Evangelist, Basilica of Saint Paul Outside the Walls in Rome

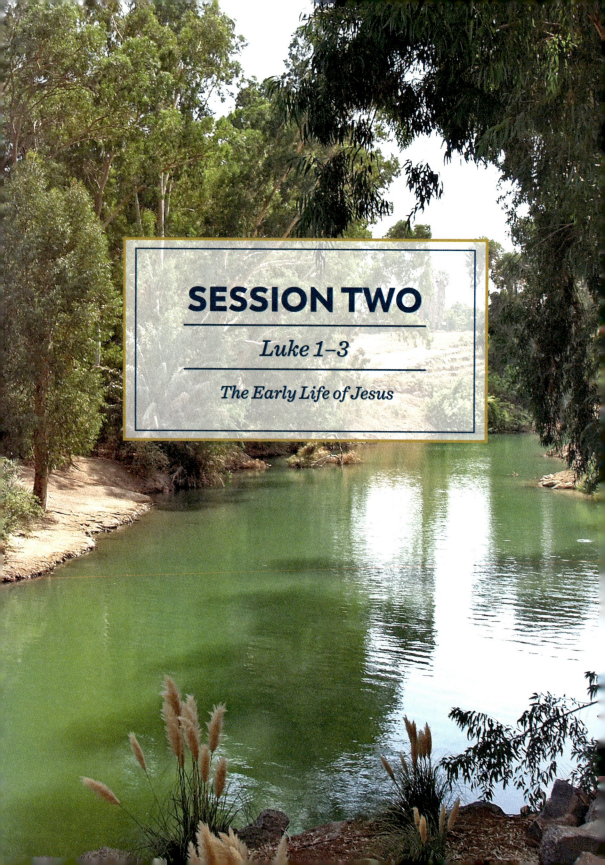

SESSION TWO

Luke 1–3

The Early Life of Jesus

HOME PREPARATION

OVERVIEW

The Beginning of Luke (Luke 1–3)

Of the four Gospels, only two, Matthew's and Luke's, tell us about Jesus' infancy and the years leading up to his public ministry. Luke's Gospel begins with the angel Gabriel's appearance to Zechariah to announce that Zechariah's wife, Elizabeth, will bear a son, John the Baptist, the herald of the Messiah. Then we read about the Annunciation, when Gabriel tells the Blessed Virgin Mary that she will bear God's Son. Later, Mary visits her cousin Elizabeth, and we witness a beautiful scene in which John leaps and dances in Elizabeth's womb—a scene that echoes the Old Testament when David danced before the Ark of the Lord (see 2 Samuel 6:16).

There are many lessons we can learn in these first chapters of Luke's Gospel, especially from the Blessed Mother. In God's unfolding plan of salvation, her role cannot be overstated. The *Catechism* explains that "in Mary, the Holy Spirit *manifests* the Son of the Father, now become the Son of the Virgin. [Mary] is the burning bush of the definitive theophany. … She makes the Word visible in the humility of his flesh" (CCC 724). This means that just as God made himself known to Moses through a burning bush (see Exodus 3), God is now made visible through Jesus. Luke's narrative shows us how this was made possible by Mary's fiat: "Let it be done to me according to your word" (Luke 1:38). Mary's yes to God's initiative helps us recognize how our own yes influences our relationship with God and his work in our lives.

In addition to the Annunciation and the Visitation, other events in these early chapters include the angel choirs rejoicing on the night of Jesus' birth, Simeon and Anna acknowledging Jesus during the Presentation, and the boy Jesus being lost for three days while he was in the Temple. These events serve as a prelude to Jesus' public ministry, and they reveal that something truly important has transpired in the narrative of salvation. Before now, God intervened in history through his prophets and other messengers—but this time, *God himself* enters history. The Lord comes among us as one of us; the one who created man and woman becomes human, all to save humanity.

This is the moment when God's promise of redemption is fulfilled!

< Jordan River

READ AND RESPOND

Below is the daily reading plan for Session Two. Each day leading up to your next small group meeting, carefully read the assigned passage from Luke's Gospel and then write your response to the discussion question.

Remember to pray before you read.
Ask the Holy Spirit to guide you through each day's reading.

Day 2

Read

Begin with "OVERVIEW: The Beginning of Luke." Then read Luke 1:1–38 (Dedication to Theophilus; The Birth of John the Baptist Foretold; The Birth of Jesus Foretold).

Respond

Luke 1 presents a parallel contrast between Zechariah and Mary. The angel Gabriel appears to both, with a similar message for each of them. How does Zechariah's reaction to Gabriel's news compare with Mary's? What is the essential difference between their responses? What are the results of their individual responses?

Day 3

Read

Luke 1:39–80 (Mary Visits Elizabeth; and Mary's Song of Praise; The Birth of John the Baptist; Zechariah's Prophecy)

Respond

Old Testament Connection: The first chapter of 1 Samuel begins with a barren woman, Hannah, praying for a son. The Lord hears her prayer, and Hannah bears Samuel, who will become a great prophet and the last judge of Israel. Read Hannah's prayer in 1 Samuel 2:1–10, and then reread Mary's words in Luke 1:46–55. In what ways are these prayers similar?

_____

_____

_____

_____

Day 4

Read

Luke 2:1–21 (The Birth of Jesus; The Shepherds and the Angels; Jesus Is Circumcised and Named)

Respond

Luke 2:6–12 depicts Jesus being born in utter poverty. When God chose to come among us, in his tremendous providence he chose to be destitute. Why do you think God's Son chose to be born in such poverty?

_____

_____

_____

_____

Day 5

Read

Luke 2:22–52 (Jesus Is Presented in the Temple; The Return to Nazareth; The Boy Jesus in the Temple)

Respond

Luke 2:41–52 describes how Mary and Joseph lost Jesus for three days after they came to Jerusalem for the feast of Passover. This story is included in the Rosary as the fifth Joyful Mystery. What are some ways in which we can lose Jesus for a time? How can we increase our joy at finding him again?

Presentation of Jesus in the Temple by unknown baroque artist

Day 6

Read

Luke 3:1–20 (The Preaching of John the Baptist)

Respond

Old Testament Connection: Jeremiah and Ezekiel were prophets before and during the time of the Babylonian Exile. Both called God's People to repentance; they also spoke of a new covenant that God would make with his people. Compare the introductions of Jeremiah and Ezekiel (Jeremiah 1:1–3; Ezekiel 1:1–3) with that of John the Baptist (Luke 3:1–6). What are some similarities between these Scripture passages? Why are such details helpful? Why do you think Luke introduces John the Baptist in this way?

Day 7

Read

Luke 3:21–38 (The Baptism of Jesus; The Ancestry of Jesus)

Respond

Reread Luke 3:21–22. Who is present during Jesus' baptism? Who (or what) is specifically mentioned? What can we learn about the nature of God from this moment in Luke's Gospel?

End Day 7 with this week's Application.

APPLICATION

Reflect

Before Jesus, the world waited anxiously for the coming of the Messiah. Instead of as a mighty warrior or ruler, as many people expected, the Messiah arrived as a vulnerable infant in a stable in Bethlehem. Jesus called the humble town of Nazareth home, and he learned the trade of his foster father, Joseph. The Son of God lived an ordinary life, and thus he sanctified ordinary life.

Commit

No matter our situation in life, we need to serve God in humility, as Mary did. The early Church Fathers sometimes spoke about how, when we hear the Word of the Lord and say yes like Mary, we allow God to be born again in our own time. Consider the areas in your life where you need to say yes to the Lord as Mary did. Let's say yes when he calls us to do something, no matter how small or great.

Pray

The Magnificat (Luke 1:46–55, NAB)

My soul proclaims the greatness of the Lord,
my spirit rejoices in God my Savior.
For he has looked with favor on his lowly servant.

From this day all generations will call me blessed:
the Almighty has done great things for me,
and holy is his Name.

He has mercy on those who fear him
in every generation.

He has shown the strength of his arm,
he has scattered the proud in their conceit.

He has cast down the mighty from their thrones,
and has lifted up the lowly.

He has filled the hungry with good things,
and the rich he has sent away empty.

He has come to the help of his servant Israel
for he has remembered his promise of mercy,
the promise he made to our fathers,
to Abraham and his children forever. Amen.

SMALL GROUP MEETING - Day 8

DISCUSS

Return to the "Read and Respond" questions from your home preparation this week and discuss your answers with the group.

WATCH

Write down your notes and reflections on the video in the space provided.

I. **Introduction: Luke 1–3, The Early Life of Jesus**

   A. Key concept moving forward: *recapitulation*

   B. Example of recapitulative history: Jesus' temptation in the wilderness

II. **The Annunciation**

   A. The perpetual virginity of Mary

   B. Power of the Most High overshadows Mary (Luke 1:35)

   C. Glory of the Lord filled the tabernacle (Exodus 40:34)

   D. Vows of self-affliction (Numbers 30)

III. **The Visitation**

   A. David bringing the Ark of the Covenant into Jerusalem (2 Samuel 6)

   B. Mary visiting Elizabeth in the hill country of Judah for three months (Luke 1:39–40)

   C. Contents of the Ark

   1. Ten Commandments: Jesus is the Word made flesh

   2. Bowl of manna: Jesus is the bread from heaven

   3. Aaron's budding rod: Jesus is the great high priest

   D. Mary is the New Ark of the Covenant

IV. **Jesus: True God and True Man**

   A. Jesus became truly man while remaining truly God (CCC 464)

   B. *Gaudium et Spes,* 22: the author of human nature lived a human life

   C. Divine condescension

      1. Jesus is the Son of God by nature

      2. We become sons and daughters of God by grace

V. **The Baptism of Jesus**

   A. Jordan River

      1. Where Jesus' public ministry begins; also where Joshua took Jericho (Joshua 4–6)

      2. Coronation: where King Solomon was anointed by a Levite (1 Kings 1:39); where Jesus was anointed by John the Baptist, a Levite (Luke 3:22)

   B. *Mikvot* (Heb., singular *mikvah*) = ritual baths

   C. In Baptism: what Jesus is by nature, we become by grace (a son or daughter of God)

VI. **Conclusion: The Universal Call to Holiness**

   A. *Lumen Gentium,* 40: we are all called to the perfection of charity, to become saints

   B. Task of the Christian: to know God and bring him to others

REVIEW

Following the video presentation (and depending on time), you can review the video with your group or read the workbook responses to Session Two's discussion questions beginning on page 113. Revisit the workbook responses on your own as you begin the home preparation for the next session.

FOR FURTHER STUDY

Luke as Historian

The Gospel of Luke is revered for being historically accurate, despite persistently skeptical scholars. One of the more famous scholars who became convinced of Luke's historical trustworthiness was the Protestant New Testament historian F.F. Bruce (1910–1990). Bruce initially approached the Gospel of Luke with some suspicion, as he was trained in the history of classical antiquity. When he was asked to lecture on applying the historical methods of classical Roman and Greek antiquity to the New Testament, he became convinced the New Testament was incredibly reliable historically and that Luke was perhaps the greatest historian from antiquity. His lectures eventually formed the core of his book *Are the New Testament Documents Reliable?* (1943), which remains in print.[4]

Luke includes a great deal of historical information and terms, and he writes in the style of historians of antiquity: "It seemed good to me also, having followed all things closely for some time past, to write an orderly account" (Luke 1:3). More than the other Gospel writers, Luke situates the events he narrates in both the Roman and the Jewish history of the time. He does not place Jesus "a long time ago, in a galaxy far, far away." Instead, he writes, "In the days of Herod, king of Judea" (Luke 1:5), "In those days a decree went out from Caesar Augustus" (Luke 2:1), and "In the fifteenth year of the reign of Tiberius Caesar, Pontius Pilate being governor of Judea, and Herod being tetrarch of Galilee, and his brother Philip tetrarch of the region of Ituraea and Trachonitis, and Lysanias tetrarch of Abilene, in the high-priesthood of Annas and Caiaphas" (Luke 3:1–2).

Skeptics have challenged Luke's reference to "the first enrollment, when Quirinius was governor of Syria" (Luke 2:2). The first-century Jewish historian Josephus informs us that Quirinius conducted a famous census sometime between AD 6 and 7.[5] This census, which included a violent revolt led by Judas the Galilean, was too late for the events surrounding Jesus' birth. Luke mentions this revolt in Acts 5:37; thus, he could be distinguishing this census from the later, more violent one; it may have been a lesser-known, more peaceful census. Another possibility is that Quirinius may have held his position, or a similar one, more than once, but there is no evidence for this. What is perhaps most likely is that we should translate the Greek word usually translated as "first" (*prōtē*) as "before" or "earlier than," which would fit how Luke uses it elsewhere (as in Acts 1:1). Most of the skeptical challenges leveled by scholars can be handled in similar ways.

◆ ❖ ◆

Mary's Perpetual Virginity

The perpetual virginity of Mary is controversial among Protestants, mainly because of the explicit mention of Jesus' brothers and sisters (e.g., Luke 8:19–21). But the earliest Protestant Reformers—Martin Luther, Ulrich Zwingli, John Calvin, and Martin Bucer—all agreed that Mary remained a virgin after Jesus' birth. Although the Gospels were written in Greek, which has many different words for familial relationships, their Jewish context must be kept in mind. In the Hebrew language, cousins, half brothers, stepbrothers, and the like would all be referred to simply as "brothers" (in Hebrew, *achim*), since this was the only word for those relations.

Luke most likely went to Mary as a primary source, and the Blessed Mother remains a special presence throughout his Gospel. Perhaps the most important testimony we have for Mary's perpetual virginity is Luke's own account of the Annunciation. Notice first that Mary is identified twice in the passage as "virgin," and both times in the same verse (Luke 1:27). In this cultural context one would expect her to be a virgin, and thus, we would not expect her to be named "virgin." If there were an exception—widow, adulterer, or harlot, for example—we might expect that to be highlighted, but not her virginity. Luke mentions not once but *twice* that she is the "virgin," and this seems to be drawing attention to the fact that this is her state in life, even in marriage.

Notice, too, what the angel Gabriel says to Mary (Luke 1:30–33):

- "You have found favor with God"
- "You will conceive in your womb"
- "You will … bear a son"
- "You shall call his name Jesus"

- "He will be great"
- "He ... will be called the Son of the Most High"
- "The Lord God will give to him the throne of his father David"
- "He will reign over the house of Jacob for ever"
- "Of his kingdom there will be no end"

Mary is "betrothed" to Joseph (Luke 1:27), although their marriage has not been completed yet. Considering that they are finishing the marriage process and will soon be living together as husband and wife, if Mary did *not* intend to remain a virgin in her marriage as before, we might ask which of the nine statements the angel makes to her should be the most surprising. Perhaps that her son will be the Son of God, "Son of the Most High" (Luke 1:32)? Another runner-up might be that he will be heir to the throne of David and have an everlasting kingdom (see Luke 1:32–33). But what would be the *least* surprising statement for a young woman in the process of getting married? That would have to be, "You will conceive in your womb" (Luke 1:31).

Espousals of Virgin Mary and St. Joseph by unknown artist, Cathedral of Our Lady, Antwerp

And yet not only is this the biggest surprise for her, but it is the only thing she questions: "How can this be, since I have no husband?" (Luke 1:34). This is a rather silly question if she intends to renounce her virginity in marriage; she must have known countless married couples who had children during their married lives. Notice, too, that the angel does not tell her *when* she will conceive, except that it is in the future tense—which implies any time between the giving of this statement and her death. If Mary does not intend to remain a virgin in marriage, having at least one child during her married life with Joseph should not come as any surprise. Her question makes sense only if she *never* intends to "know a man" (as the Greek reads literally), even in marriage.

This explains the contrast between her surprise and Zechariah's. Zechariah is surprised that God could work a miracle. Mary does not yet know about the miraculous birth; instead, she is concerned about having to break what must have been her prior vow of virginity. Why would God ask her to break her promise to him? The angel explains that it will be God's miracle: "The Holy Spirit will come upon you, and the power of the Most High will overshadow you" (Luke 1:35). In this, Mary does not have to worry about breaking her vow. She does not have to "know a man," for the Holy Spirit will accomplish the conception.

It is also important to notice that the book of Numbers in the Old Testament has an entire chapter devoted to important vows. Key among them are vows a woman might make "to afflict herself" (Numbers 30:13). Old Testament legal scholars tell us such vows of self-affliction can pertain to fasting from certain food or drink or abstaining from marital relations. That this passage concerns marital relations becomes clear when it says that if the husband accepts the vow his wife took but then changes his mind, he is guilty, and she is not (see Numbers 30:15). This only makes sense with marital relations, since none of the other forms of abstinence involve both the husband and the wife.

This seems to be the sort of vow Mary took, which Joseph must have accepted, for the husband who "says nothing to her from day to day ... establishes all her vows, or all her pledges, that are upon her; he has established them, because he said nothing to her on the day that he heard of them" (Numbers 30:14).

✦ ❖ ✦

Mary as the New Ark of the Covenant

Luke was very careful and intentional when he composed his Gospel. One way we see this is in his depiction of Mary as the new Ark of the Covenant. This is evident in the subtle parallels he draws between the Visitation and the Old Testament account of King David bringing the Ark of the Covenant to Jerusalem (2 Samuel 6). In Luke 1:39–56, Mary, Elizabeth, and John the Baptist are all foils for David, underscoring Mary's identity as the new Ark.

The key is the Greek translation of 2 Samuel 6. Most of the New Testament, including the Gospel of Luke, was originally written in Greek. When the New Testament authors quoted from the Old Testament, they frequently referenced the most common Greek translation, known as the Septuagint. If we pay careful attention to this Greek translation of 2 Samuel 6, we find the following parallels with Luke's account of the Visitation:

The Meeting of Mary and Elisabeth by Carl Heinrich Bloch

Old Testament (2 Samuel 6)	New Testament (Luke 1)
"**David arose and went** with all the people who were with him *from* **Baale-Judah** to bring up ... the ark of God" (2 Samuel 6:2).	"In those days **Mary arose and went** with haste into the hill country, *to* a city of **Judah**" (Luke 1:39).
When David sees what happens to Uzzah, he asks, "How **can the ark of the Lord come to me?**" (2 Samuel 6:9), and David initially *refuses* to take the ark with him.	When Elizabeth sees Mary, she asks, "And why is this granted me, that **the mother of my Lord should come to me?**" (Luke 1:43), and Elizabeth *welcomes* Mary into her home.
Then "the ark of the Lord **remained** in the house of Obed-edom the Gittite **three months**" (2 Samuel 6:11).	"And Mary **remained** with her [Elizabeth] about **three months**" (Luke 1:56).
When David brought the ark back to Jerusalem, he "**danced** before the Lord with all his might. ... David [was] **leaping** and **dancing** before the Lord" (2 Samuel 6:14, 16).	"And when Elizabeth heard the greeting of Mary, the child **leaped** in her womb; ... she [Elizabeth] exclaimed ..., 'When the voice of your greeting came to my ears, the child in my womb **leaped** for joy'" (Luke 1:41, 42, 44).

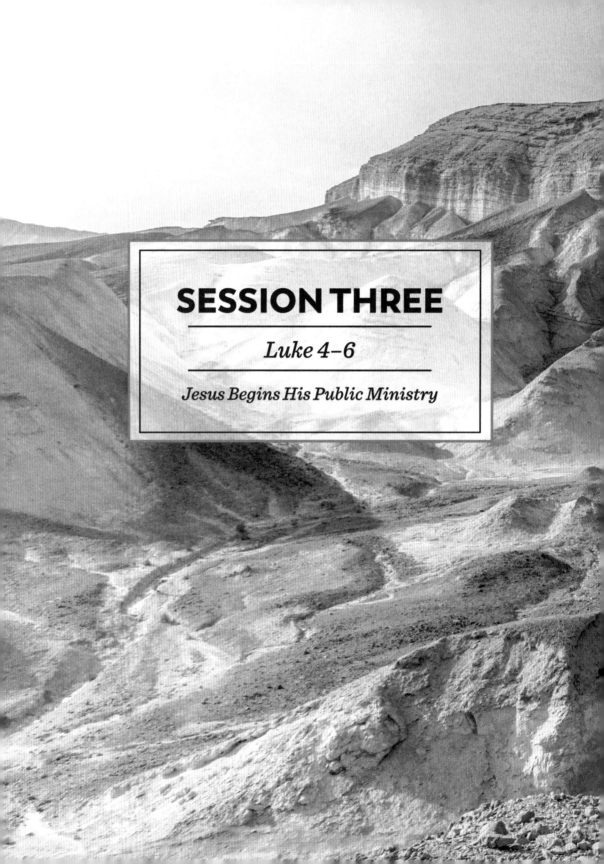

HOME PREPARATION

OVERVIEW

Preaching and Teaching (Luke 4–6)

The opening chapters of Luke's Gospel form what is known as the infancy narrative. Luke 1:5–2:52 contains a collection of stories about Jesus' birth and childhood that offers us snapshots of his early life. After the account of Jesus getting lost in the Temple, the infancy narrative in Luke ends by saying that "Jesus increased in wisdom and in stature, and in favor with God and man" (Luke 2:52). Luke's Gospel then pivots from Jesus' childhood to his baptism in the Jordan River, a definitive moment that signals the start of his public ministry.

How does Jesus' ministry begin? Luke tells us that after Jesus is baptized and anointed by the Holy Spirit, his first act is to go into the wilderness to fast, pray, and battle with the Devil. This provides a fundamental model of the Christian life. At our baptism, we, too, are anointed by the Holy Spirit; as we journey through the "wilderness" of our life, we fast, pray, and battle temptation. Our own public ministry—serving others, sharing the Good News, and leading people to Jesus—must flow from our relationship with God, which is strengthened through the disciplines of fasting and prayer.

After his time in the wilderness, Luke tells us that Jesus travels through the region of Galilee preaching, teaching, and healing. While Jesus is celebrated by some, he is rejected by others. He comes into direct conflict with the religious authorities on multiple occasions. This is in part because the Jewish leaders of his day were focused on extending the laws of the Old Covenant that separated the People of God from other nations. When God gave Israel these laws, it was so they could become a holy nation, a people "set apart"—but what the religious authorities didn't understand was that it was ultimately to prepare Israel to become a blessing to the other nations, fulfilling the covenantal promise God had made to Abraham (see Genesis 22:16–18). In his teaching, Jesus points to the perfection of the Law and its true fulfillment, revealing God's mercy.

Ultimately, as his teachings through the Sermon on the Plain demonstrate, Jesus wants his followers to be holy, like God—and he's showing them how to live by that holiness and share it with others.

< Judean Desert

READ AND RESPOND

Below is the daily reading plan for Session Three. Each day leading up to your next small group meeting, carefully read the assigned passage from Luke's Gospel and then write your response to the discussion question.

Remember to pray before you read.
Ask the Holy Spirit to guide you through each day's reading.

Day 9

Read

Begin with "REVIEW: Preaching and Teaching." Then read Luke 4:1–30 (Temptation of Jesus; Jesus Begins Preaching and Teaching in Galilee; the Rejection of Jesus at Nazareth).

Respond

Old Testament Connection: The prophecy recorded in Isaiah 61 refers to "the year of the LORD's favor" ("the acceptable year of the Lord" in Luke 4:19). This is the Sabbath year (Year of Jubilee), during which slaves were to be released and the land would rest and be restored. Read Isaiah 61. How does this passage relate to the scene in Luke 4:14–30? What is significant about Jesus' teaching, and how do his listeners respond?

Temptation of Jesus, fresco, Antwerp

Day 10

Read

Luke 4:31–44 (The Man with an Unclean Spirit; Healings at Simon's House; Jesus Preaches in the Synagogues of Judea)

Respond

Why does Jesus so frequently go to deserted places, as he does in Luke 4:42? What significance does this hold for our personal prayer lives?

_____

_____

_____

_____

Day 11

Read

Luke 5:1–16 (Jesus Calls the First Disciples; Jesus Cleanses a Leper)

Respond

In Jesus' day, it was customary to fish at night on the Lake of Gennesaret. In Luke 5:1–11, we find that Simon Peter and his companions have fished all night without success. Jesus tells them to try one more time; in obeying him, they catch a multitude of fish. Why does this lead Simon Peter to exclaim, "Depart from me, for I am a sinful man, O Lord" (Luke 5:8)?

_____

_____

_____

_____

Day 12

Read

Luke 5:17–39 (Jesus Heals a Paralytic; Jesus Calls Levi; The Question About Fasting)

Respond

Skeptics sometimes claim that Jesus never said, "I am God." Yet not only are there are many places where he affirms his divine identity when asked (as in Mark 14:61–62); he also says and does things that make it clear he is claiming to be God. Reread Luke 5:20–26. How do Jesus' words and actions here demonstrate his claim to be God?

_____

_____

_____

_____

Day 13

Read

Luke 6:1–26 (A Teaching About the Sabbath; The Man with a Withered Hand; Jesus Chooses the Twelve Disciples; Jesus Teaches and Heals; Blessings and Woes)

Respond

Across the Gospels: Compare Matthew 5:1–12 and Luke 6:20–26. What are some of the differences between these accounts?

_____

_____

_____

_____

Day 14

Read

Luke 6:27–49 (Love for Enemies; Judging Others; A Tree and Its Fruit; Hearers and Doers)

Respond

Carefully read Luke 6:27–36. If we are called to imitate God, what does Jesus' command here tell us about God?

_____

_____

_____

_____

End Day 14 with this week's Application.

Jesus Teaches the People by the Sea by James Tissot

APPLICATION

Reflect

Jesus' commandment to love is so central to the Christian life, and yet it is so difficult. One of the hardest teachings he gives us is to love our enemies. Jesus explains the obvious: "If you love those who love you, what credit is that to you? For even sinners love those who love them" (Luke 6:32). Of course, the point of the command is not to earn credit or score points but to become more like God. In loving others—including our enemies, those who wish us harm or do us harm—we find Jesus' call to "be merciful [i.e., forgiving], even as your Father is merciful" (Luke 6:36).

Commit

Take a moment in silent prayer and ask God to bring to your mind a person who, for whatever reason, you do not get along with or for whom you harbor negative feelings. Without justifying the actions of someone who has caused you harm, take a moment and say a prayer for them, a prayer for their good, since God loves everyone.

Pray

Jesus, I thank you for your love for me.
Thank you for forgiving me again and again.
Help me to live with and love the people in my life better.
Help me to learn to love as you do.
Right now, I pray for those I consider enemies in the present and in my past.
I ask that you draw them closer to you and bless them. Amen.

SMALL GROUP MEETING - Day 15

DISCUSS

Return to the "Read and Respond" questions from your home preparation this week and discuss your answers with the group.

WATCH

 Session Three: Luke 4–6

Write down your notes and reflections on the video in the space provided.

I. Introduction: Luke 4–6, Jesus Begins His Public Ministry

II. Temptation in the Wilderness

    A. Jesus, the faithful Son

    B. Recapitulates the history of Israel

    C. Israel in the wilderness for forty years, tried and tempted

    D. Jesus in the wilderness for forty days, tried and tempted

    E. Satan strikes at the *identity* of Christ (Luke 4:9)

    F. Three forms of piety: prayer, fasting, almsgiving

III. Rejection at Nazareth

    A. Challenges of being a disciple

    B. "Acceptable year of the Lord": Year of Jubilee (Luke 4:18–19)

    C. Heart of Jesus' ministry = freedom from bondage (sin)

    D. Jesus shares Old Testament stories

        1. Stories where the hero is not Israel, but Gentiles

        2. Listeners turned against him

        3. Following Jesus' model when facing opposition

IV. **Sermon on the Plain**

   A. Pharisees: ones who are separated (holy)

   B. Mosaic covenant set the Jewish people apart from other nations

   1. Set apart so they can learn to follow God

   2. The point: called to bring God to the other nations

   C. Laws of ritual and moral holiness (Leviticus 19): in the sermon, Jesus shows the perfection of the Law

   D. Universal call to holiness and universal call to evangelize all people

V. **The Beatitudes**

   A. Logic of love

   B. The exterior life is an overflow of the interior life

   1. *Ashrei* (Heb.), *makarios* (Gk.): "happy"

   2. Beatitudes = the key to a happy life

   C. The new Mount Sinai: the new giving of the Law

VI. **Conclusion: Love of Neighbor**

REVIEW

Following the video presentation (and depending on time), you can review the video with your group or read the workbook responses to Session Three's discussion questions on page 117. Revisit the workbook responses on your own as you begin the home preparation for the next session.

FOR FURTHER STUDY

The Early Church and the Old Testament Community of Israel

As Brant Pitre has shown, Jesus bases his community, the Church, on a pattern already found in the Old Testament—as we see in Exodus 24:[6]

Exodus	Luke
Moses represents God	Jesus is God
Aaron is Moses' high priestly representative	Peter is Jesus' high priestly representative
Aaron and the brothers Nadab and Abihu are three set apart	Peter and the brothers James and John are three set apart
Twelve pillars represent the Twelve Tribes	Twelve apostles represent the Twelve Tribes
Seventy elders	Seventy followers sent out

The Sanhedrin of Jesus' day, which represented the Jewish leadership composed of Sadducees and Pharisees, was based on this Israelite community structure. The Sanhedrin was likewise presided over by a high priest and was composed of seventy members. It seems likely that the Sanhedrin recognized that Jesus was setting up an alternative community, a "new Israel," and this created some of the tension between the Sanhedrin and Jesus.

Ordaining of the Twelve Apostles by James Tissot

Echoes of the Royal Household

Jesus preaches about the Kingdom of God throughout Luke; the phrase appears more than thirty times. In these chapters of Luke, we see Jesus showing us what that kingdom looks like through his teaching and healing. He also begins to establish the Kingdom of God on earth with the calling of the twelve apostles (Luke 6:12–16). In this, Luke once again alludes to the Old Testament.

In 1 Kings 4, we find King Solomon, a son of David, organizing his kingdom with twelve royal officers who are responsible for the feeding of the royal household. In a parallel way, Jesus, the Son of David, organizes his kingdom by appointing twelve of his own officers, the apostles. This holds great significance for us today as members of God's household because the apostles' successors, our bishops and priests, continue to feed us through the sacraments.

HOME PREPARATION

OVERVIEW

"Who Is This?" (Luke 7–9)

Luke tells us that from the moment the Devil departs from Jesus in the wilderness, Jesus returns to Galilee and gets straight to work. He travels to the synagogues, preaching the Good News. He calls his first disciples and, thanks to his teachings and healings, gains a crowd of followers. As the Gospel progresses, Jesus' teachings become more challenging, and his miracles become more dramatic. Many people—John the Baptist's followers, Herod, the religious leaders, the crowds of Jews, the Gentiles, and even Jesus' own disciples—are all asking variations of the same question: "Who is this?"

Right away we see that Jesus has much in common with the Old Testament prophets, particularly in his miraculous healings. In Jesus' healing of the centurion's slave, we find a parallel to the prophet Elisha when he healed Naaman the Syrian (see 2 Kings 5). When Jesus raises the widow's son at Nain, it echoes Elijah's raising of the widow's son at Zarephath (see 1 Kings 17). These healings not only meet the desperate physical needs of those who come to Jesus; they also serve as prophetic signs. Through them, those who have eyes to see will recognize who he is.

But Jesus is more than a prophet. Even as he proclaims the Kingdom of God, Jesus' actions call to mind certain members of the royal house of David. King Solomon composed wisdom literature and proverbs; in Jewish tradition, he was also associated with exorcisms.[7] Thus, as the people receive Jesus' own wisdom in parables and witness his exorcisms, they begin to see in Jesus the new son of David, the long-expected royal heir to David's throne: the Christ who was to come into the world.

Jesus himself asks his disciples the more important question: "Who do *you* say I am?" Immediately after Peter acknowledges that Jesus is "the Christ of God," Jesus describes the suffering he will undergo in Jerusalem: he will be rejected, suffer greatly, and be killed before rising on the third day. In this, he also links his coming death with discipleship: he tells his disciples, "If any man would come after me, let him deny himself and take up his cross daily and follow me." The cost of discipleship is high. We cannot be disciples on our own; it is impossible. But we aren't on our own: Jesus leads the way. If we, like Peter, acknowledge that Jesus is the Christ, the Son of God, we must be willing to follow his lead.

READ AND RESPOND

Below is the daily reading plan for Session Four. Each day leading up to your next small group meeting, carefully read the assigned passage from Luke's Gospel and then write your response to the discussion question.

*Remember to pray before you read.
Ask the Holy Spirit to guide you through each day's reading.*

Christ and the Centurion by Paolo Veronese

Day 16

Read

Begin with "OVERVIEW: 'Who Is This?'" Then read Luke 7:1–17 (Jesus Heals a Centurion's Slave; Jesus Raises a Widow's Son at Nain).

Respond

How does the centurion's response to Jesus (Luke 7:1–10) underscore his great faith? How can you apply this lesson in your life?

Day 17

Read

Luke 7:18–50 (Messengers from John the Baptist; A Sinful Woman Forgiven)

Respond

In Luke 7:18–23, we read about how John the Baptist sent two of his followers to Jesus, asking if he really was the one "who is to come" or if they should "look for another" (Luke 7:19). What are we to make of Jesus' response?

_____

_____

_____

_____

Jesus Raises the Widow's Son from Nain by unknown artist
11th century, illuminated manuscript

Day 18

Read

Luke 8:1–25 (Some Women Accompany Jesus; The Parable of the Sower; The Explanation of the Parable; A Lamp Is Not Hidden; The True Kindred of Jesus; Jesus Calms a Storm on the Sea)

Respond

1. Women were somewhat ostracized in antiquity. They were even barred from serving as witnesses in many ancient courtrooms. With that in mind, what does Luke 8:1–3 tell us about Jesus and his relationship with women?

2. What conclusions can be drawn from Luke's account of Jesus' calming the storm on the sea (Luke 8:22–25)?

The Penitent Magdalen by Georges de La Tour

Day 19

Read

Luke 8:26–56 (Jesus Heals the Gerasene Demoniac; A Girl Restored to Life and a Woman Healed)

Respond

Notice the reaction of many people after Jesus heals the Gerasene demoniac (Luke 8:26–39). The pig herders and those living in the region ask Jesus to depart from them and go somewhere else. This might strike us as odd at first, but their reaction makes sense from a human perspective. All those pigs—their livelihood—were destroyed. In what ways might we react in a similar way to Jesus?

Note: This is a very personal question. Consider jotting down some notes to take to prayer, but avoid sharing responses to this question during your small group discussion.

Day 20

Read

Luke 9:1–27 (The Mission of the Twelve; Herod's Perplexity; Feeding the Five Thousand; Peter's Declaration That Jesus Is the Christ; Taking Up One's Cross)

Respond

1. *Old Testament Connection:* Read 1 Kings 17:8–24. What similarities do you notice between Jesus and Elijah?

2. In Luke 9:10–17, we read how Jesus works a miracle by feeding more than five thousand people with a few loaves of bread. How does this relate to the mystery of the Eucharist?

Day 21

Read

Luke 9:28–62 (The Transfiguration; Jesus Heals a Boy with a Demon; Jesus Again Foretells His Death; True Greatness; Another Exorcist; A Samaritan Village Refuses to Receive Jesus; Would-Be Followers of Jesus)

Respond

It is very difficult to follow Jesus. In Luke 9:57–62, Jesus meets several would-be followers who are caught between their desire to follow Jesus and earthly matters. How do their dilemmas relate to concerns you face in your own life, and how is Jesus calling you to surrender these concerns to him? Also, earlier in Luke, Jesus explains that any who wish to follow him must take up their crosses daily (Luke 9:23). What crosses can you voluntarily take up as part of your Christian life?

End Day 21 with this week's Application.

APPLICATION

Reflect

When Jesus asks his disciples "Who do the people say that I am?" (Luke 9:18), Peter famously responds, "The Christ of God" (Luke 9:20). But who do *you* say Jesus is? If, like Peter, you believe him to be the Christ, ask yourself two questions:

- Does my behavior reflect that I believe Jesus is the Christ?
- What can I do to make my life reflect better that I truly believe that Jesus is the Christ?

Commit

Our relationship with God requires us to extend God's love to others, in particular those whom we encounter every day. Spend a few minutes asking God to help you come up with one concrete way to extend God's love to someone important in your life—for example, a spouse, a child, a neighbor, or a coworker.

Pray

Jesus, thank you for your tremendous love. Increase my faith.
Help me love you more. Help me love others as you love them.
Make me a vessel of your love for everyone I encounter in my daily life. Amen.

SMALL GROUP MEETING - Day 22

DISCUSS

Return to the "Read and Respond" questions from your home preparation this week and discuss your answers with the group.

> *Note:* As mentioned above, the question for Day 4 is personal, and participants should keep their responses private. Avoid sharing responses to this question in the group.

WATCH

 Session Four: Luke 7–9

Write down your notes and reflections on the video in the space provided.

I. **Introduction: Luke 7–9, The Mission and Miracles of Jesus**

II. **The Bible and the Mass**

    A. "I am not worthy" (Luke 7:6–9)

        1. Jesus marvels at the centurion's faith

        2. The centurion recognizes that Jesus' authority is not limited by time or space

    B. *Lex orandi, lex credendi*: how we pray affects how we believe

III. **The Healing Power of Jesus**

    A. Gerasene demoniac

        1. Possessed by multiple (a legion of) demons

        2. "Return to your home" (Luke 8:39): Jesus sends man back to his family

    B. Hemorrhaging woman

        1. *Tzitzit* (Heb., tassel), *kanaph* (Heb., wing): both worn at the corner of the garment

2. Malachi 4:2: "the sun of righteousness shall rise, with healing in its wings [*kanaph*]"

3. The woman understands the messianic background of Malachi 4:2

IV. **Feeding of the Five Thousand**

   A. Multiplication of the bread: Eucharistic themes

   B. Formula: takes, blesses, breaks (Luke 9:16)

   1. Last Supper (Luke 22:19)

   2. Emmaus account (Luke 24:30)

V. **The Papacy in Scripture**

   A. Jesus transformed the Davidic kingdom into the Church (Luke 9:20, Matthew 16:16)

   B. Authority to bind and loose

   1. Importance of keys: linked to Isaiah 22:22–24

   2. *Al habayit* (Heb.), the one in charge when the king is away (prime minister)

   3. Recapitulation of Isaiah 22: the one with the keys

   C. Peter, the Rock = foundation of the Church

   D. *Eben shetiyah* (Heb.), cornerstone of the world

VI. **Conclusion: The Importance of the Magisterium**

   A. *Catechism of the Catholic Church*, compendium of teachings of the Church

   B. Magisterium, teaching authority of the Catholic Church

REVIEW

Following the video presentation (and depending on time), you can review the video with your group or read the workbook responses to Session Four's discussion questions beginning on page 121. Revisit the workbook responses on your own as you begin the home preparation for the next session.

FOR FURTHER STUDY

Titles for Jesus

Luke uses many titles for Jesus in his Gospel. If we take some of them in turn, we can better understand the significance of each:

- **Son of Man.** Considering its Old Testament context, it seems with this title that Jesus has his messianic status in mind as the anointed of God who comes to redeem his people. We see this especially in Daniel 7:13–14: "Behold, with the clouds of heaven there came one like a son of man, and he came to the Ancient of Days and was presented before him. And to him was given dominion and glory and kingdom ...; his dominion is an everlasting dominion." Jesus invokes this passage concerning himself when he is before the Sanhedrin: "From now on the Son of man shall be seated at the right hand of the power of God" (Luke 22:69).

- **Son of God.** The title "Son of God" emphasizes Jesus' divinity, and this is, of course, true. It is also a reference to Jesus as the messianic heir to the throne of King David, since the heirs of David's line were understood in some way to be sons of God, inspired by the language of the Psalms, where God declares the king to be his son (Psalm 2:7).

- **Christ or Messiah.** "Christ" and "Messiah" are the same title in different languages: *Christos* in Greek, *Mashiach* in Hebrew. Both mean "anointed one." In the Old Testament, anyone anointed with oil, like a king, was identified as a *mashiach* ("anointed one"). Eventually, as with the prophets, we find an expectation of one to come who will be anointed by God. This is the Messiah who would come and redeem God's People.

- **Son of David.** Jesus is the legitimate heir to King David's throne. The Son of David was understood to be the Messiah, the Christ, who was the heir to David's throne and would rule David's kingdom.

- **Lord.** The Greek "Lord," as Jesus is called in the New Testament, was the translation of the word *Adonai* (Heb., "Lord"), used by Jews in place of speaking God's name ("Yahweh").

- **King of the Jews.** This is implied by the title Son of David. "King of the Jews" was also the term used by the Roman soldiers to mock Jesus (Luke 23:37) and the mocking inscription placed on the Cross (Luke 23:38).

♦ ❖ ♦

The Samaritans

Samaritans are mentioned throughout Luke's Gospel, including Luke 9:51–56 and in the parable of the Good Samaritan (Luke 10:29–37). But who were the Samaritans?

Samaritans were not Jews, but they could be considered Israelites. They were descendants of the ten northern tribes of Israel. In the Bible, 2 Kings 17 recounts the Assyrian conquest of Samaria and how, when the Assyrians came to control the Northern Kingdom, they forced intermarriage among five different groups of Gentiles.

As the books of Ezra and Nehemiah recount, the Samaritans emerged as rivals of the Southern Kingdom of Judah (comprising the tribes of Judah, Benjamin, and Levi) after the Jews returned from the Babylonian Exile and rebuilt Jerusalem and the Temple. Notable differences between the Samaritans and the Jews centered on what they considered Scripture and where they worshipped. The Samaritan Scriptures comprised only the first five books of the Bible, and their texts differed in some places from the Jewish Torah. In addition, Samaritans worshipped at their temple on Mount Gerizim, whereas Jews worshipped at the Temple in Jerusalem.

At the dawn of the first century AD, Samaritans defiled the Temple in Jerusalem, and Jews and Samaritans saw themselves not as neighbors but as enemies. The Samaritans who eventually follow Jesus are a sign that Jesus is uniting all Israel, which had been divided since the death of King Solomon.

Kykkos Monastery, Cyprus. Mosaic. Good Samaritan.

Women in Luke

Many women in Luke's Gospel play important roles in Jesus' public ministry:

Mary, Jesus' Mother: Luke's Gospel places a strong emphasis on Mary, more than any other Gospel with the possible exception of John. We hear about the Annunciation of the angel Gabriel to Mary (Luke 1:26–38). We read about Mary's visit to Elizabeth (Luke 1:39–56). We hear how Mary "kept all these things in her heart" and how Jesus, the Lord of heaven and earth, was "obedient" to Mary (Luke 2:51).	**Elizabeth:** Luke's Gospel begins with John the Baptist's mother, Elizabeth, who is described as "righteous before God, walking in all the commandments and ordinances of the Lord blamelessly" (Luke 1:6). God grants her the blessing of a child even though she has remained barren into old age. At the Visitation, Elizabeth receives the hidden mystery of the Incarnation (Luke 1:43–44) and remains with Mary, our Lord's mother.
Anna: She is a prophetess and a member of the tribe of Asher, one of the ten lost tribes of Israel from the north. Anna fasts and prays in the Temple day and night and is an early proclaimer of the Good News about Jesus (Luke 2:36–38).	**Simon Peter's Mother-in-Law:** In Luke 4:38–39, we read about Jesus healing Simon Peter's mother-in-law. As soon as her illness leaves her, she rises and serves Jesus and those with him.
A Widow in Nain: Jesus sees a widow in Nain whose son has died. Out of compassion for her—and perhaps looking ahead to when his own mother, a widow, will watch him die—Jesus raises the widow's son from the dead (Luke 7:11–17).	**A Sinful Woman Who Anoints Jesus' Feet:** An unnamed woman who is known as a sinner anoints the feet of Jesus. Jesus uses the opportunity to publicly declare that her sins are forgiven because of her great love (see Luke 7:36–50).

Mary Magdalene: She is one of Jesus' prominent female disciples. We see her in Luke 8:2 as one of the women who provide support for Jesus' ministry, and in Luke 24:10 we read that she is one of the women who find Jesus' tomb empty.	**Joanna:** She is the wife of Chuza, the steward of King Herod, and is also counted among Jesus' female disciples. Joanna contributes to and supports Jesus' ministry (Luke 8:3). She is also present at the empty tomb (Luke 24:10).
Susanna: She is a female disciple who provides for his ministry (Luke 8:3).	**Jairus' Daughter:** Jairus is a synagogue official whose daughter has died. Jesus raises her from the dead (Luke 8:52–56).
The Woman with the Hemorrhage: A woman in the crowd who has had an incurable hemorrhage for many years touches Jesus to be healed, and he declares her healed because of her faith (Luke 8:43–48).	**A Widow Who Gives All She Has:** In Luke 21:2–4, Jesus tells of a poor widow who gives all she has as an offering, using her as example of generosity.

There are other, unnamed women in Luke's Gospel, but the women above are key figures who appear at significant moments throughout Jesus' ministry. They show us that Jesus held women in high esteem, affirmed their dignity, and encouraged others to look to them as examples of discipleship. When he rose from the dead, women were the first preachers of the Good News of the Resurrection.

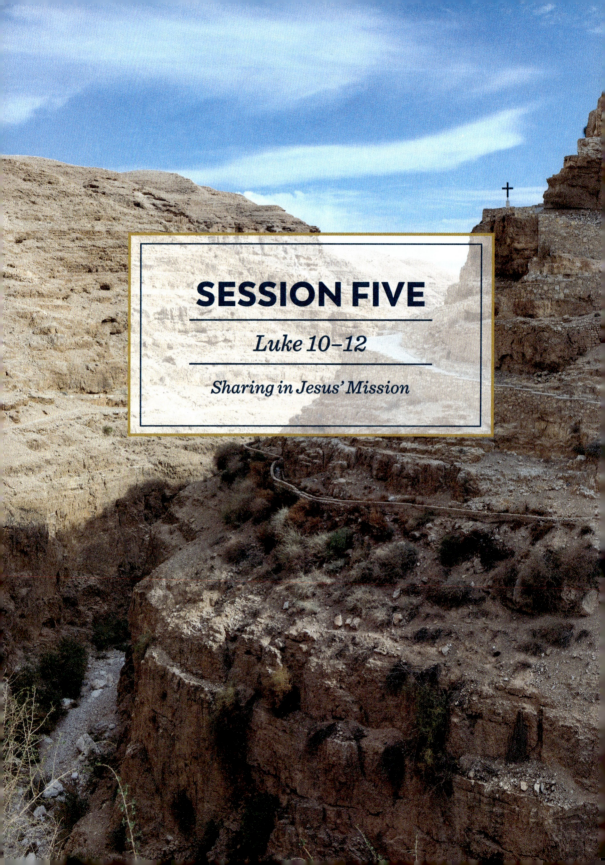

HOME PREPARATION

OVERVIEW

Treasures of the Kingdom (Luke 10–12)

Peter's confession that Jesus is "the Christ of God" (Luke 9:20) marks a turning point in Luke's narrative. From now on, Jesus turns his gaze toward Jerusalem—the place where all things will ultimately be fulfilled.

While Jesus continues to teach the growing crowds and perform healings, he also sends out his followers in pairs—seventy in all—as laborers for the harvest, proclaiming the Kingdom of God to the surrounding regions. This is an important point in Jesus' public ministry. Mirroring the Jewish Sanhedrin, which is made up of seventy members, Jesus' seventy disciples go out to invite the nearby towns into the community of God's kingdom. As modern followers of Jesus, we inherit this call of missionary discipleship: we must go out to invite our neighbors into God's kingdom. And who are our neighbors? As Jesus teaches in the parable of the Good Samaritan, there can no longer be any social barriers. All people are our neighbors; no one is excluded.

The religious leaders challenge Jesus, and Jesus continues to point out their lack of understanding. He contrasts the righteousness that the Kingdom of God requires with the hypocrisy of the Pharisees, Sadducees, and scribes of "this generation" (Luke 11:31). While the religious authorities are overly concerned with external matters, Jesus highlights the importance of our disposition of heart. It may be easy for us to cast a judgmental gaze on the religious leaders who completely missed the point—but we, too, need to guard against pride and hypocrisy. We must heed Jesus' message in our own lives, making sure that our example does not keep others away from God's kingdom.

In these chapters of Luke, Jesus resumes the teaching that he began in the Sermon on the Plain, sharing with his followers how they are to pray, how to persevere in prayer, and what true blessedness means. Jesus' message is both comforting and challenging. He wants to share the treasure of God's kingdom with everyone willing to seek it—but acquiring this treasure requires something of us. It requires giving up our self-reliance and trusting in God. It requires *doing* what is right, not just having nice intentions. It requires being attentive in our spiritual life and watchful against temptation.

It can all be summed up in one line: seek God and his kingdom first, and the treasure will be yours.

< Wadi Qelt

READ AND RESPOND

Below is the daily reading plan for Session Five. Each day leading up to your next small group meeting, carefully read the assigned passage from Luke's Gospel and then write your response to the discussion question.

*Remember to pray before you read.
Ask the Holy Spirit to guide you through each day's reading.*

Day 23

Read

Begin with "OVERVIEW: Treasures of the Kingdom." Then read Luke 10:1–24 (The Mission of the Seventy; Woes to Unrepentant Cities; The Return of the Seventy; Jesus Rejoices and Thanks the Father).

Respond

Jesus often prays to God the Father, and in this chapter of Luke, we see Jesus thanking God the Father. In what ways can we adopt a posture of gratitude when conversing with our heavenly Father? Why is giving thanks an essential attitude for prayer?

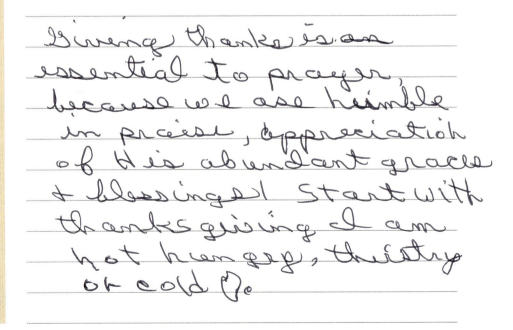

Giving thanks is an essential to prayer, because we are humble in praise, appreciation of His abundant grace + blessings. I start with thanksgiving I am not hungry, thirsty or cold.

Christ in the House of Martha and Mary by Johannes Vermeer

Day 24

Read

Luke 10:25–42 (The Parable of the Good Samaritan; Jesus Visits Martha and Mary)

Respond

Old Testament Connection: After the old kingdom of Israel split in two, conflicts between the rebellious northern tribes dwelling in Samaria (Israel) and the southern tribes near Jerusalem (Judah) went on for generations. Each saw the other as enemies. During the reign of King Ahaz of Judah, Israel took captive two hundred thousand men from Judah. Read about this conflict and its interesting outcome in 2 Chronicles 28:8–15. What connections can you find between this passage and Jesus' parable of the Good Samaritan (Luke 10:29–37)?

Day 25

Read

Luke 11:1–26 (The Lord's Prayer; Perseverance in Prayer; Jesus and Be-elzebul; The Return of the Unclean Spirit)

Respond

Across the Gospels: Read Matthew 6:9–13; then reread Luke 11:2–4. What are the differences between the Lord's Prayer in Matthew and the Lord's Prayer in Luke? In what ways are they similar?

Holy Eucharist - okay most importance

Day 26

Read

Luke 11:27–54 (True Blessedness; The Sign of Jonah; The Light of the Body; Jesus Denounces the Hypocrisy of the Pharisees and Lawyers)

Respond

Jesus is often harsher when dealing with the Pharisees and scholars of the law than he is with the ordinary sinners who come to him. What might account for this?

Wealth + pride of rich prevents asking god for their forgiveness

The Parable of the Rich Fool by Rembrandt

Day 27

Read

Luke 12:1–34 (A Warning Against Hypocrisy; Whom to Fear; The Parable of the Rich Fool; Do Not Be Anxious)

Respond

Consider Jesus' words: "Where your treasure is, there will your heart be also" (Luke 12:34). Where is your heart? In other words, what do you treasure above all else? What are some ways you can turn away from the "treasures" of the world and align your heart with the treasure of God's kingdom?

False gods are an evil deception by Satan, anything we think about more than praise God.

Day 28

Read

Luke 12:35–59 (The Necessity of Watchfulness; The Faithful and the Unfaithful Servant; Jesus the Cause of Division; Interpreting the Present Time; Settling with Your Accuser)

Respond

What makes Jesus a source of "division" (Luke 12:49–53)? What does this tell us about the cost of discipleship?

> Satan wants to divide & attack, separate us!

End Day 28 with this week's Application.

The Lord's Prayer by James Tissot

APPLICATION

Reflect

Do you ever get anxious or worried? Take a moment to think through what worries you. Then spend some time reflecting on God's love for you. In his Gospel, Luke makes clear to the reader that God is here for us; he loves us and wants to guide us closer to him. Remember: God is a loving Father who is all-powerful, knows everything, and wants what is best for you.

Commit

Jesus sent out the seventy with a mission. Spend some time each day praying about the mission God has for you. Pray for the grace of the Holy Spirit to help you understand God's plan and vocation for you. Have you already found your vocation? If so, what is something concrete God is asking you to do to live out your vocation better?

Pray

The Lord's Prayer

(Luke 11:2–3)

Father, hallowed be your name.

Your kingdom come.

Give us each day our daily bread;

and forgive us our sins,

for we ourselves forgive every one who is indebted to us;

and lead us not into temptation. Amen.

SMALL GROUP MEETING - Day 29

DISCUSS

Return to the "Read and Respond" questions from your home preparation this week and discuss your answers with the group.

WATCH

 Session Five: Luke 10–12

Write down your notes and reflections on the video in the space provided.

I. **Introduction: Luke 10–12, Sharing in Jesus' Mission**

II. **The Good Samaritan**

　A. Parables: an effective teaching tool for a rabbi

　B. *Mitzvah* (Heb.): a good deed

　C. The parable is a reversal: combines love of neighbor with love of enemy

　　1. The Samaritan in the parable demonstrated a selfless love of neighbor

　　2. C.S. Lewis, *The Four Loves* (book): *philia, storge, eros, agape*

III. **Jesus Sends Out His Disciples**

　A. "It's your turn": seventy disciples sent out to share the works of Jesus

　B. Observing Jesus in prayer

　　1. *Lectio divina*: scriptural reading, meditation, and prayer

　　2. The Lord's Prayer (Luke 11:2–4)

　　3. Jesus' example of prayer; relationship between prayer and public life (see CCC 2602)

IV. The Sign of Jonah

- A. Jonah in the belly of fish (Jonah 1:17) linked with Jesus buried in the belly of the earth for three days (Luke 24:7)

- B. Jesus calls Peter Simon, son of *Jonah* (Matthew 16:17)

    1. *Yonah* (Heb.): dove

    2. Comparing Jonah and Peter

        a. Jonah 1–4: Jonah leaves Joppa and eventually preaches repentance to the Gentiles (Ninevites), leading to their conversion

        b. Acts 10:1–48: Peter leaves Joppa and preaches repentance to the Gentiles (Cornelius and family), leading to their conversion

- C. A reference for our universal call to evangelize

V. Forgiveness

- A. Martyrdom of St. Stephen (Acts 7:55–56)

- B. Forgiveness is willing the good of others

- C. Blasphemy against the Holy Spirit (CCC 1864)

    1. Deliberately refusing to accept God's mercy

    2. Rejecting forgiveness and the salvation offered by the Holy Spirit

VI. Conclusion: The Mercy of God

- A. Grace of the Sacrament of Reconciliation (Confession)

- B. Extending love and forgiveness to others (Matthew 18:21–22, Luke 17:3–4)

REVIEW

Following the video presentation (and depending on time), you can review the video with your group or read the workbook responses to Session Five's discussion questions beginning on page 125. Revisit the workbook responses on your own as you begin the home preparation for the next session.

FOR FURTHER STUDY

The Kingdom of God

From where does Jesus pull his concept of the "Kingdom of God" in the Gospel of Luke (and the other Gospels)? There is no expression "Kingdom of God" in the Old Testament. The two closest ideas are the kingdom that God establishes as detailed in Daniel 2:44 and the Kingdom of Yahweh (the Kingdom of the Lord) mentioned in 1 and 2 Chronicles (see, for example, 1 Chronicles 28:5; 2 Chronicles 13:8).

In Daniel, we find the interpretation of the Babylonian king Nebuchadnezzar's dream pertaining to earthly kingdoms that will arise in the future. At the end, Daniel, inspired by the Spirit of God, explains that God himself will set up a kingdom that will be everlasting. In 1 and 2 Chronicles, the Kingdom of the Lord is identified as the Kingdom of David, which God promised would be everlasting.

When Jesus preaches that the Kingdom of God or the Kingdom of Heaven is at hand, most of his listeners naturally make these connections to the Jewish Scriptures. And what the Scriptures reveal is that this kingdom is, in Jesus, none other than the fulfilled Davidic kingdom, which God himself is establishing through the Messiah, the Son of David.

In the New Testament Gospels, this theme takes on an even deeper meaning as we see the Kingdom of God as a heavenly kingdom administered on earth through Jesus and his Apostles. In Luke, the theme of the Kingdom of God is tied to the Resurrection of Christ. The Kingdom of God is an everlasting kingdom, ruled by a King (Jesus) who defeats death. We can find this theme paralleled in Luke's other work, the Acts of the Apostles, where Peter's preaching contrasts King David, who is dead, with Jesus, the King who has triumphed over death (see Acts 2:29–32).

All human kings who have ruled earthly kingdoms have died—but Jesus is the eternal King who rose from the dead and rules eternally from his heavenly throne. This is a prominent theme in the Gospel of Luke, bound with the invocation "your kingdom come" (Luke 11:2) in the Lord's Prayer.

♦ ❖ ♦

The Parable of the Good Samaritan

The parable of the Good Samaritan is an important point in Jesus' teaching, when he begins to be challenged by his audience: "And who is my neighbor?" (Luke 10:29). Here Jesus implicitly combines the command to love one's neighbor with the command to love one's enemy.

The Samaritans and Jews were bitter enemies at the time of Jesus. They were both descendants of the people of Israel: The Jews were descendants of the southern tribes of Judah (after whom they were named) and Benjamin, and the uncounted priestly tribe of Levi, which had returned from the Babylonian Exile. The Samaritans were descendants of the northern Israelites, the ten lost tribes of Israel.

At the dawn of the first millennium, the Samaritans had defiled the Jewish Temple in Jerusalem. This was the main point of contention between the two communities. For the Jews, the one temple was the Temple in Jerusalem; Samaritans, in contrast, believed the one temple was their temple at Mount Gerizim, in the north.

The Good Samaritan by Pieter Lastman

When Jesus tells the parable about the Good Samaritan, to Jewish ears it sounds something like "the good terrorist" or "the good enemy." In the parable, the priest and Levite both pass by the injured man. Perhaps they are (understandably) frightened for their own physical safety, imagining that the robbers are still close by. But despite his own fears, the Samaritan heroically helps the injured man, presumably a Jew, his "enemy." He makes the sacrifice to help him, care for him, and take him to the safety of an inn, where he pays for his care and healing.

Jesus gives this example of what it means to love your neighbor, and he tells his listeners to "go and do likewise" (Luke 10:37).

❖

"Daily Bread"

The Greek phrase *epiousios*, which is used only in the Gospels of Matthew and Luke and only in the context of the Lord's Prayer (CCC 2837), has puzzled translators and interpreters from antiquity to today. It is often translated as "daily" and can be taken as a reference to the manna in the wilderness, which God provided every day to the freed Israelites on their journey to the Promised Land (see Exodus 16).

It is also understood as the "bread for tomorrow," for the day at the end of time. In addition, St. Jerome translated it once as "supersubstantial" (in Latin), based on a more literal reading of the Greek—which, if broken down etymologically, means "above" (*epi* in Greek; *super* in Latin) and "nature" (*ousios* in Greek; *substantia* in Latin). This would make it a reference to our supernatural bread.

All these connotations point to the Eucharist, which this petition can be understood to reference. The Eucharist is our daily bread here and now, on our pilgrimage to the true promised land of heaven. And it is our "bread for tomorrow"—for eternal life. Finally, the Eucharist is our supernatural food.

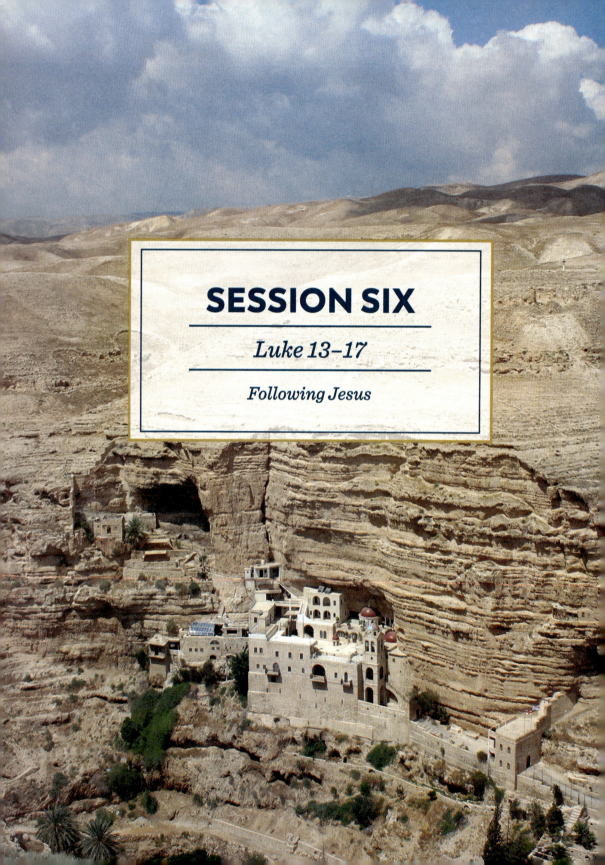

HOME PREPARATION

OVERVIEW

Counting the Cost (Luke 13–17)

In all that Luke has recorded so far, Jesus has upended everyone's expectations of who the Messiah is. Jesus bears the power of God—but instead of crushing the enemies of the Jewish people, he heals the sick and frees those bound by Satan. Jesus speaks with God's moral authority—but he breaks bread with sinners and criticizes religious leaders. Jesus teaches with an inverted logic, saying things like "he who is least among you all is the one who is great" (Luke 9:48) and "love your enemies" (Luke 6:27). But those with ears to hear recognize that the kingdom has come into their midst.

At this stage in Luke's narrative, Jesus continues to make his way to Jerusalem, teaching the multitudes about the Kingdom of God through parables. This teaching method was commonly used by Jewish teachers in Jesus' day; famous rabbis often taught using parables. In these chapters of Luke, we encounter one parable after another. Some are famous beyond the Christian Faith, while others are more inscrutable in their meaning—but the shared beauty of these parables is that they reveal the heart of God. Three parables in particular—the parables of the lost sheep, the lost coin, and the prodigal and his brother—teach us that God will never stop pursuing us; he longs for us to turn back to him. The more closely we read these parables, the more we see what Jesus is trying to communicate: God's love for us, sinners though we are, is boundless.

This leads us to ask, How well do we love God in return? How far are we willing to go to follow him? Jesus does not shy away from saying what, exactly, the cost of discipleship is. In Luke he explicitly says that unless you hate your earthly life, unless you carry your own cross, you cannot be his disciple.

This is important for us to remember. In the barest terms, being Jesus' disciple means, quite simply, losing your life—which is, paradoxically, the only way to preserve it. If we call ourselves Jesus' disciples, we must ask, How much are we willing to give in order to follow him? If our answer isn't "everything," then anything else we do will, in the end, fall short. As we reflect on Jesus' parables and teachings in this part of Luke's Gospel, let us keep in mind what it means to give God our everything.

< Monastery of St. George in Wadi Qelt

READ AND RESPOND

Below is the daily reading plan for Session Six. Each day leading up to your next small group meeting, carefully read the assigned passage from Luke's Gospel and then write your response to the discussion question.

Remember to pray before you read.
Ask the Holy Spirit to guide you through each day's reading.

Day 30

Read

Begin with "OVERVIEW: Counting the Cost." Then read Luke 13:1–17 (Repent or Perish; The Parable of the Barren Fig Tree; Jesus Heals a Crippled Woman).

Respond

In an earlier chapter of Luke's Gospel, Jesus teaches a parable about trees and fruit: "For no good tree bears bad fruit, nor again does a bad tree bear good fruit; for each tree is known by its own fruit" (Luke 6:43–44). In the parable of the barren fig tree, Jesus tells the fate of a tree that bears *no* fruit (Luke 13:6–9). How are these teachings related?

Jesus' Parable of the Barren Fig Tree

Day 31

Read

Luke 13:18–35 (The Parable of the Mustard Seed; The Parable of the Leaven; The Narrow Door; The Lament over Jerusalem)

Respond

What does the parable of the leaven (Luke 13:20–21) tell us about the Kingdom of God?

Parable of the Great Banquet by Brunswick Monogrammist

Day 32

Read

Luke 14 (Jesus Heals the Man with Dropsy on the Sabbath; Humility and Hospitality; The Parable of the Great Banquet; The Cost of Discipleship; About Salt)

Respond

Across the Gospels: Read Matthew 5:13; then reread Luke 14:34–35. Why does Jesus bring up the importance of salt retaining its taste? How is this a metaphor for the Christian life?

Day 33

Read

Luke 15 (The Parable of the Lost Sheep; The Parable of the Lost Coin; The Parable of the Prodigal and His Brother)

Respond

What does the parable of the lost sheep (Luke 15:1–7) tell us about God?

_____

_____

_____

_____

_____

Parable of the Lost Sheep by unknown artist

Day 34

Read

Luke 16 (The Parable of the Dishonest Steward; The Law and the Kingdom of God; The Rich Man and Lazarus)

Respond

In the parable of the dishonest steward (Luke 16:1–13), the master commends the dishonest steward for how he acted. What point is Jesus trying to make here? How should we interpret his advice to "make friends for yourselves by means of unrighteous mammon" (Luke 16:9)? How does this relate to his following words: "He who is faithful in a very little is faithful also in much" (Luke 16:10) and "You cannot serve God and mammon" (Luke 16:13)?

The Rich Man and Lazarus by School of Frans Francken

Day 35

Read

Luke 17 (Some Sayings of Jesus; Jesus Cleanses Ten Lepers; The Coming of the Kingdom)

Respond

Old Testament Connection: After the death of King Solomon, ten tribes of Israel rebelled and broke away, dividing the kingdom into two: the Northern Kingdom in Samaria (known as Israel) and the Southern Kingdom near Jerusalem (known as Judah). The Samaritans of Jesus' day were the remnant of the breakaway group and dwelled separately from the Jews. With this context in mind, reread Luke 17:11–19. What is so significant about this scene? Specifically, why ten, and why does Luke emphasize the detail about the Samaritan who returned?

End Day 35 with this week's Application.

APPLICATION

Reflect

When Jesus cleansed the ten lepers, only one came back to thank him. How often do you pause to thank God for the ways in which he acts and intervenes in your daily life? How can you be more intentional in offering thanks to God throughout the day?

Commit

Commit to examining your conscience every night before going to bed. Spend just a few minutes asking the Holy Spirit to guide you in thinking back through your day. In what ways did you allow his grace to guide you throughout the day? Thank him for that. In what ways did you perhaps fail to love God, your family, or your neighbor? Offer an Act of Contrition to God for the moments you fell short. Finally, come up with one small practical resolution for living love better the next day.

Pray

Jesus, you tell us that we find you in those around us.
The Two Great Commandments, to love you and to love our neighbor,
are so closely related. Help me to see the needs of the others in my midst
and to serve those needs in love. Jesus, I love you. Amen.

SMALL GROUP MEETING - Day 36

DISCUSS
Return to the "Read and Respond" questions from your home preparation this week and discuss your answers with the group.

WATCH

 Session Six: Luke 13–17

Write down your notes and reflections on the video in the space provided.

I. Introduction: Luke 13–17, Following Jesus

II. Understanding the Parables of Jesus

    A. Asking the Holy Spirit to guide personal discernment of parable stories: "What does this parable have to say to me?"

    B. Messianic quality to Jesus' parables

        1. Connection to the teachings of Solomon, son of David

        2. *Mashalim* (Heb.): wise sayings, proverbs (Gr. translates as "parables")

III. The Cost of Discipleship

    A. Rabbi invited a disciple with a formulaic statement

        1. *Lech acharai* (Heb.): "Come, follow me"

        2. Goal of discipleship: become like the master

    B. Fan vs. follower

    C. Pick *up* your cross (see Luke 14:27), not pick *out* your cross

    D. Dietrich Bonhoeffer, *The Cost of Discipleship*

IV. The Divine Banquet

    A. Covenant: sacred means of extending family relationships by swearing oaths

B. Marriage: a metaphor for our relationship with God (wedding feast of the Lamb)

C. Meal parables prepare us for the Last Supper

1. New Covenant instantiated in (represented by) Jesus' Body and Blood

2. Sacrifice of the Cross poured out in an unbloody way

3. We are present at the wedding feast here on earth

V. **The Prodigal Son**

A. Major theme in Scripture: exile and return, going away and coming back

B. Interior conversion: understanding the heart of the Father

C. Younger brother called to conversion; older brother called to love like the father

VI. **Conclusion: Prayerfully Reading Scripture**

A. Inhabit the text of Scripture

B. Discover yourself as a character in the story

C. Understanding text historically and personally

REVIEW

Following the video presentation (and depending on time), you can review the video with your group or read the workbook responses to Session Six's discussion questions beginning on page 129. Revisit the workbook responses on your own as you begin the home preparation for the next session.

FOR FURTHER STUDY

The Parable of the Prodigal Son (Luke 15:11–32)

The theme of two brothers is well known in the Old Testament—Cain and Abel, Isaac and Ishmael, Jacob and Esau. Jesus tells the parable of the Prodigal Son precisely because he is being challenged by the "righteous" about why he is spending time with "sinners."

In the parable, the elder brother clearly stands in for these "righteous" critics, while the prodigal stands for the "sinners." Jesus' point is not merely the salvation of the sinners who repent; even more, it is about the abundant and merciful love of God for his people. Through this parable, one of the richest in the Gospel of Luke and found only in his Gospel, we see the loving mercy of God made manifest, as it has clearly been shown in Jesus' public ministry of healing and having fellowship with sinners. Jesus has not come to condemn the unrighteous but to offer them—to offer us—salvation.

Jesus ends his parable with the complaint of the elder son not only to underscore his mercy but also to warn his critics. In the parable, the elder son is blind; he cannot see how he falls short of the father's abundant love. The Pharisees and scribes, like the elder son, need to recognize their own weaknesses and lack of love. The invitation before them is to become like the loving father of the parable. Such love goes beyond mere "box-checking"; it instead reaches to the core of forgiving those who trespass against us.

The Parable of the Rich Man and Lazarus (Luke 16:19–31)

This is a fascinating parable because, in it, we don't find the rich man actively hurting anyone or committing harm. He just ignores Lazarus, the beggar in his midst. The rich man's sin is simply neglect. Jesus is teaching us that we are accountable not just for our actions but also for our lack of action—our failure to reach out in love and service to others. As James writes, "Whoever knows what is right to do and fails to do it, for him it is sin" (James 4:17).

When the rich man descends to the underworld after death, he suffers torment on behalf of his sins of omission and asks that someone be sent back from the dead to warn his relatives. The response he receives is instructive: if they did not believe the Torah and the prophets, even someone rising from the dead would not convince them.

We might think this is only about Jesus' impending Resurrection. However, in John 11 we find another Lazarus who dies and is raised from the dead. In that account, we find the words from Luke's parable proved a reality: rather than coming to believe in the power of Jesus, his adversaries decide to try to kill both Lazarus and Jesus (John 12:9–10).

The Rich Man and the Poor Lazarus by Hendrick ter Brugghen

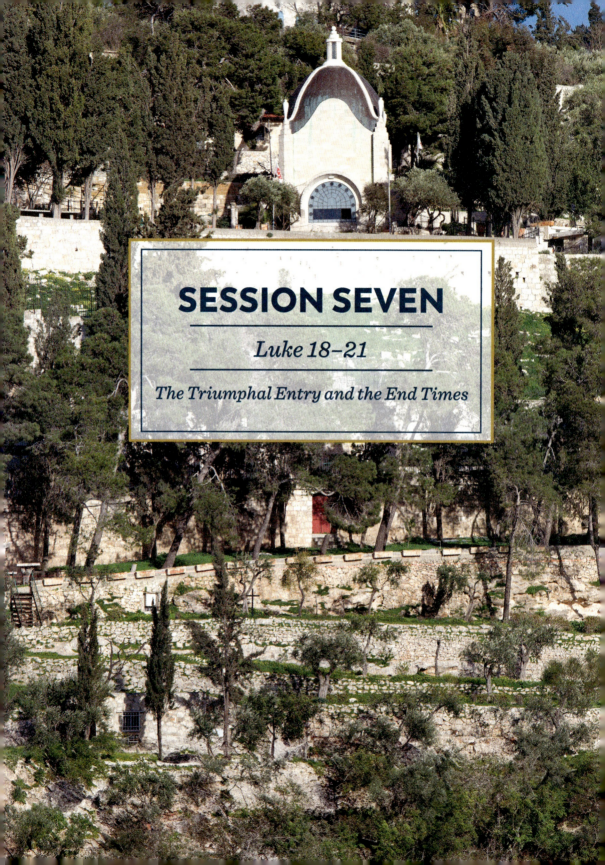

HOME PREPARATION

OVERVIEW

The Final Approach (Luke 18–21)

Jesus and his disciples have been traveling through Galilee, Samaria, Judea, and the surrounding regions for about three years. Throughout the journey, Jesus has demonstrated the Kingdom of God and professed the salvation of those who repent and come to him in faith, fulfilling his mission as "the Son of man" who has come "to seek and to save the lost" (Luke 19:10). Now, in these chapters of Luke's Gospel, Jesus and his disciples make their final approach to Jerusalem.

After Jesus' triumphant entry into the city, Luke recounts how Jesus' last days unfold. Jesus cleanses the Temple, chasing out the corrupt sellers. He confronts hostile religious leaders who try to trap him over and over again with their questions, and he sets their own traps against them. He weeps over Jerusalem, foretelling not only his own death and Resurrection but also the coming destruction of the Temple and the fall of Jerusalem. It's all quite dramatic.

In this penultimate section of Luke's Gospel, we can learn much from how Jesus interacts with the people. With those who are vulnerable and in need—sinners, outcasts, the infirm, and children—Jesus meets them where they are, extending healing, comfort, and forgiveness to those who repent. Jesus also meets those who come at him with hostile intent—namely, the Pharisees, Sadducees, and scribes—with assertiveness and authority, calling out their contradictions. As we read about these interactions, the challenge lies in choosing which ones we will emulate: Will we be like those who bring their infants to Jesus, like the blind beggar of Jericho, or like Zacchaeus, the chief tax collector—people who grasp the significance of the moment, who understand who Jesus truly is and seek him out? Or will we continually confront Jesus and challenge his teachings in our hearts like the religious leaders?

For now the time when God walks among his people as one of them has nearly passed. These pages of Luke's Gospel reveal the growing storm that will lead directly to Judas Iscariot's betrayal and Jesus' arrest. As Jesus teaches in the Temple and the hostilities of the religious leaders come to a head, Luke finally sets the stage for the main event, when "everything that is written of the Son of man by the prophets will be accomplished" (Luke 18:31).

◁ Sanctuary of Dominus Flevit on the Mount of Olives

READ AND RESPOND

Below is the daily reading plan for Session Seven. Each day leading up to your next small group meeting, carefully read the assigned passage from Luke's Gospel and then write your response to the discussion question.

Remember to pray before you read.
Ask the Holy Spirit to guide you through each day's reading.

Day 37

Read

Begin with "OVERVIEW: The Final Approach." Then read Luke 18 (The Parable of the Widow and the Unrighteous Judge; The Parable of the Pharisees and the Tax Collector; Jesus Blesses the Children; The Rich Ruler; A Third Time Jesus Foretells His Death and Resurrection; Jesus Heals a Blind Beggar near Jericho).

Respond

In what ways does the parable of the widow and the unrighteous judge (Luke 18:1–8) reflect our relationship with God? What are the crucial differences between the judge and God?

Christ with the Children by Sébastien Bourdon

Day 38

Read

Luke 19:1–27 (Jesus and Zacchaeus; The Parable of the Ten Pounds)

Respond

What can we learn from Zacchaeus, a tax collector who clearly cheated people, and his conversion upon encountering Jesus (Luke 19:1–10)?

_____

_____

_____

_____

The Entry of Christ into Jerusalem by Félix Louis Leullier

Day 39

Read

Luke 19:28–48 (Jesus' Entry into Jerusalem; Jesus Weeps over Jerusalem; Jesus Cleanses the Temple)

Respond

Old Testament Connection: As King David neared the end of his life, he took certain steps to confirm the path of succession for his son Solomon. Read 1 Kings 1:32–40; then reread Luke 19:33–40. What similarities do you notice between these two scenes? How is this moment yet another confirmation of Jesus' identity?

Day 40

Read

Luke 20:1–18 (The Authority of Jesus Questioned; The Parable of the Wicked Tenants)

Respond

How does the parable of the wicked tenants (Luke 20:9–19) relate to Jesus' conflicts with the religious leaders of Israel?

Day 41

Read

Luke 20:19–47 (The Question About Paying Taxes; The Question About Man's Resurrection; A Question About the Messiah; Jesus Denounces the Hypocrisy of the Scribes)

Respond

Religious Context: In Jesus' day, the Sadducees were a Jewish sect that represented the priestly aristocracy. Unlike the Pharisees, the Sadducees believed that only the first five books of Moses (the Torah) were God's divinely inspired Word. They did not accept doctrines such as the resurrection of the dead or the existence of angels.

Reread Luke 20:27–40. How are the Sadducees, who don't believe in the resurrection, trying to trap Jesus? How does Jesus effectively dismantle their trap?

Day 42

Read

Luke 21 (The Widow's Offering; The Destruction of the Temple Foretold; Signs and Persecutions; The Destruction of Jerusalem Foretold; The Coming of the Son of Man; The Lesson of the Fig Tree; Exhortation to Watchfulness)

Respond

How can we apply Jesus' point about the widow's offering (Luke 21:1–4) to our own lives?

_____

_____

_____

_____

End Day 42 with this week's Application.

The Destruction of the Temple of Jerusalem by Francesco Hayez

APPLICATION

Reflect

Jesus praises the poor widow for her meager offering, for she gives freely from what little she has, from her poverty. We often judge others and ourselves by the world's standards, but Jesus is teaching us not to focus on what someone has (or does not have) or what someone is able to give. He asks us instead to make love our aim, to give freely and completely without holding back. In what ways can you give yourself freely and completely to God?

Commit

Zacchaeus wanted to see Jesus so desperately that he climbed a tree. Think about one way you can resolve to spend a little more time with Jesus each day to better "see" him in your life. Perhaps you can set aside a few minutes of quiet prayer before starting to work. Perhaps you can reserve a set time each day to read Scripture. Perhaps you can attend daily Mass a few times a week (or more). Commit to living this out not just for the remainder of this Bible study but in your daily life after this study ends.

Pray

The *Suscipe* Prayer of St. Ignatius of Loyola

Take, Lord, and receive all my liberty, my memory,
my understanding, and my entire will—all that I have and possess.
You have given all to me. To you, O Lord, I return it.
All is yours. Dispose of it wholly according to your will.
Give me only your love and your grace, for this is sufficient for me. Amen.

SMALL GROUP MEETING - Day 43

DISCUSS

Return to the "Read and Respond" questions from your home preparation this week and discuss your answers with the group.

WATCH

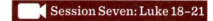 Session Seven: Luke 18–21

Write down your notes and reflections on the video in the space provided.

I. Introduction: Luke 18–21, The Triumphal Entry and the End Times

II. The Triumphal Entry of Jesus into Jerusalem

   A. Jesus fulfills Zechariah's prophecy about the donkey (Zechariah 9:9); Jesus: the new Solomon, new son of David

   B. Transubstantiation

      1. Transformation of bread and wine into Christ's Body and Blood, Soul and Divinity

      2. The appearances of bread and wine remain

   C. Jesus weeps over Jerusalem

      1. "Behold, your house is forsaken and desolate" (Matthew 23:38)

      2. Ezekiel 11:23: prophecy of the presence of God going from the Temple and moving to the Mount of Olives

   D. Jesus cleanses the Temple

      1. *Tamid* (Heb.): perpetual sacrifice

      2. Jesus is preparing for a new offering, a new Lamb of God

III. The Rich Young Ruler

   A. Parable about attachments in our lives

B. Discipleship requires a total offering to Christ; detachment transforms us and our relationship with God

IV. **The Repentance of Zacchaeus**

A. Zacchaeus: chief tax collector at Jericho, defrauding people

B. Zacchaeus eats a meal with Jesus and converts; conversion requires action, not just sentiment

V. **The End Times**

A. *Parousia* (Gr.): the second coming of Jesus Christ

B. Luke 21: language foretells the destruction of the Temple, the end of the Old Testament era, the Roman invasion of Jerusalem; early Christians obeyed Jesus' warning of the signs

C. Jews understood the Temple as a microcosm of the world

D. Apocalypse

1. *Apokálupsis* (Gr.): manifestation, appearance

2. Connected to a Jewish wedding ceremony and unveiling of the bride

3. Parallel of the Bride (the Church) being unveiled to the groom (Christ)

VI. **Conclusion: Preparing for the End**

A. Importance of preparing to meet Christ at Mass and at the end of life

B. Joyful anticipation

REVIEW

Following the video presentation (and depending on time), you can review the video with your group or read the workbook responses to Session Seven's discussion questions beginning on page 133. Revisit the workbook responses on your own as you begin home preparation for the next session.

FOR FURTHER STUDY

The "Son of David" and the Use of Parables

Parables are related to proverbs. While a proverb is a short saying that conveys a common truth or pithy advice, a parable is a short "everyday" story that expresses eternal truths. In Hebrew, the word "proverbs" (*mishle*) is closely connected to "wise sayings" (*mashalim*); both are often translated into Greek as "parables" (*parabole*).

Much of the wisdom literature in the Bible, including the book of Proverbs, is attributed to King David's son Solomon. King Solomon is widely associated with proverbs and wisdom sayings. In a parallel way, Jesus is identified as the "Son of David" (Luke 18:38–39), and he primarily teaches the crowds through parables.

◆ ❖ ◆

Psalm 110: Jesus as the Divine Royal High Priest

Psalm 110 is the Old Testament passage most often quoted in the New Testament. It is also one of only two passages from the Old Testament that mention the mysterious figure of Melchizedek, the priest-king who blesses Abram in Genesis 14:17–20. In Psalm 110:4 we read, "You are a priest for ever according to order of Melchizedek." This line makes an implicit connection between priesthood and kingship, since Melchizedek is described in Genesis 14:18 as a "priest of God Most High" and the "king of Salem" (a place that later receives the new name Jerusalem).

When Jesus uses this passage in Luke's Gospel, though, he focuses on the first verse. Jesus asks his audience, who had been trying to trap him, "How can they say that the Christ is David's son? For David himself says in the Book of Psalms, 'The Lord said to my Lord, Sit at my right hand, till I make your enemies a stool for your feet.' David thus calls him Lord; so how is he his son?" (Luke 20:41–44).

In the Judaism of Jesus' day, this psalm was understood messianically; Melchizedek was clearly seen as a messianic figure. However, it was not clear in Second Temple Judaism that the Messiah would be God himself visiting his people. Jesus is trying to point out the divine nature of this Melchizedekian royal high priest: although a descendant of David and thus the "Son of David," he is David's "Lord" because he is none other than the Lord himself.

SESSION EIGHT

Luke 22–24

The Death, Resurrection, and Ascension of Jesus

HOME PREPARATION

OVERVIEW

The Last Word (Luke 22–24)

This is it! We have come to the finale of Luke's Gospel. Jesus has entered Jerusalem, teaching daily in the Temple. The corrupt leaders question him, determined to destroy him. The conspiracy to kill Jesus comes to fruition as Judas Iscariot, with Satan in his heart, goes to the chief priests to betray him.

At the Last Supper, Jesus inaugurates his kingdom by sealing the New Covenant with the sacrifice of his Body and Blood. At this final Passover meal, we find Jesus stepping into this Old Testament observance, transforming it into the messianic banquet of the Lamb of God. It is here that Jesus' sacrifice, offered for our salvation, truly begins.

Following Judas' betrayal, Jesus is placed on trial before the Sanhedrin. The temporal high priest confronts the true and eternal high priest: God himself. Jesus then faces Pilate, the Roman governor of Judea, and Herod, the titular king of Judea. These encounters result in the death sentence of the God-man. Jesus is condemned and crucified.

But death does not have the last word; love does. It is a love stronger than death. Fulfilling all that the Scriptures foretold, Jesus' apparent defeat is his triumph. As Jesus explains to his disciples after his Resurrection, through his Passion and death, the sins of all are forgiven, and we are raised to new life in heaven.

What the two disciples encounter on their way to Emmaus is what we encounter in the Mass. As the disciples walk with him, Jesus explains the Scriptures to them; later, at table with them, he breaks the bread. In the same way, at Mass we celebrate the Liturgy of the Word, where we enter the Scriptures, and the Liturgy of the Eucharist, where we encounter Christ in the breaking of the bread. The Mass not only places us within the narrative of Scripture; it brings us to heaven and places Christ's life within us.

The Gospel of Luke, like all of Scripture, is ordered to this end, the meeting place between God and us. In the last words of Luke's Gospel, as the disciples return to Jerusalem in joy, we see where our journey as disciples—and the journey of our Church—begins.

< Church of Holy Sepulchre, Jerusalem

READ AND RESPOND

Below is the daily reading plan for Session Eight. Each day leading up to your next small group meeting, carefully read the assigned passage from Luke's Gospel and then write your response to the discussion question.

Remember to pray before you read.
Ask the Holy Spirit to guide you through each day's reading.

Day 44

Read

Begin with "OVERVIEW: The Last Word." Then read Luke 22:1–34 (The Conspiracy to Kill Jesus; The Preparation of the Passover; Jesus Institutes the Eucharist; The Dispute About Greatness; Peter's Denial Foretold).

Respond

Old Testament Connection: Exodus 24 recounts how God established a covenant with Israel through Moses while they were at Mount Sinai. The covenant was sealed with a sacrifice. Read about this event in Exodus 24:5–11; then reread Luke 22:19–20. What similarities do you notice between these two passages?

Day 45

Read

Luke 22:35–71 (Purse, Bag, and Sword; Jesus Prays on the Mount of Olives; The Betrayal and Arrest of Jesus; Peter Denies Jesus; The Mocking and Beating of Jesus; Jesus Before the Council)

Respond

Old Testament Connection: Daniel lived during the Babylonian Exile, serving in the court of the Babylonian king Nebuchadnezzar. Daniel received many prophetic and apocalyptic visions. Read the imagery of one such vision in Daniel 7:13–14; then reread the scene about Jesus before the chief priests and scribes in Luke 22:66–70. How do you interpret Jesus' comments to the council? How do they parallel Daniel 7?

Christ on the Mount of Olives by German School

Day 46

Read

Luke 23:1–25 (Jesus Before Pilate; Jesus Before Herod; Jesus Sentenced to Death)

Respond

Historical Context: Herod Antipas, son of Herod the Great, was the tetrarch who ruled over the region of Galilee at the time of Jesus. Herod's family was not ethnically Jewish; he descended from the Idumean converts to Judaism during the time of the Maccabean revolt. Reread Luke 23:6–9. With this context in mind, what is the irony behind Jesus' confrontation with Herod?

Day 47

Read

Luke 23:26–56 (The Crucifixion of Jesus; The Death of Jesus; The Burial of Jesus)

Respond

Across the Gospels: There are three "last sayings" of Jesus in Luke's Gospel (Luke 23:34, 43, 46). These three last sayings are not found in the other Gospels. What do these words spoken by Jesus from the Cross tell us about him?

Day 48

Read

Luke 24:1–35 (The Resurrection of Jesus; The Walk to Emmaus)

Respond

How does the story of the disciples on the road to Emmaus (Luke 24:13–35) mirror what happens during the Catholic Mass?

Day 49

Read

Luke 24:36–53 (Jesus Appears to His Disciples; The Ascension of Jesus)

Respond

Why might Jesus' ascension (Luke 24:50–51) be considered both a joyous and a sorrowful event?

End Day 49 with this week's Application.

APPLICATION

Reflect

The disciples who encountered the risen Jesus on the road to Emmaus recognized Jesus in the breaking of the bread (see Luke 24:30–31). How does your experience of the Mass help you recognize Jesus? What are some ways you can get more out of the Mass?

Commit

The Eucharist is "the source and summit of the Christian life," as the Second Vatican Council teaches (CCC 1324, quoting *Lumen Gentium,* 11). Consider one way you can strengthen your Eucharistic devotion. Maybe it is to attend Mass more frequently, twice a week (or more). Maybe you can prepare for Mass better by praying over the readings for the day. Perhaps you can use a missal or another tool to help you pay attention and recollect what you received at Mass. Perhaps you can pray more prayers of spiritual communion throughout the day. Or maybe you can visit Jesus in the tabernacle apart from Mass once or more each week or spend a set time in Eucharistic Adoration. Whatever it is, commit to living out this Eucharistic practice to foster deeper intimacy with Jesus.

Pray

Lord, help me to find you in the "bread from both tables":
in the Word of God and in the Blessed Sacrament, the Eucharist.
Whenever I open the pages of Scripture, help me to seek your face in its pages.
Whenever you are present in the Eucharist, help me to seek union with you,
the union I desire with my whole heart. Amen.

SMALL GROUP MEETING - Day 50

DISCUSS

Return to the "Read and Respond" questions from your home preparation this week and discuss your answers with the group.

WATCH

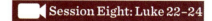 Session Eight: Luke 22-24

Write down your notes and reflections on the video in the space provided.

I. **Introduction: Luke 22–24, The Death, Resurrection, and Ascension of Jesus**

II. **The Last Supper**

  A. Passover is the central redemptive event in Old Testament

   1. Celebrated freedom from bondage in Egypt

   2. John the Baptist identifies Jesus as the "Lamb of God"

   3. Genesis 22: Abraham's sacrifice of Isaac, God will provide the lamb (*Yahweh yireh*)

  B. The Last Supper transforms Passover into the first Mass

   1. Jesus offers himself to us in an unbloody way, in a way we can receive

   2. Freedom not from Egypt but from sin

   3. At Mass, the sacrifice is re-presented

  C. Luke 22:20: the New Covenant (Jeremiah 31:31–37, Exodus 24); the Eucharist is the great source of grace, gift of God's life in us

III. The Passover and the Eucharist

A. "New Moses" bringing in a new Passover (Deuteronomy 18:15)

B. Jesus completes the sacrifice of the Passover on the Cross

   1. "It is finished": final words to end Passover celebration

C. The Eucharist is the thanksgiving offering

   1. *Vayikra Rabbah* 9:7: when the Messiah comes, all sacrifices will cease except the thanksgiving offering (the Eucharist)

IV. Open Eyes and Burning Hearts

A. Peter's denial of Jesus

B. Barabbas: false messianic claimant

   1. *Bar Abba* (Ar.): son of the father

   2. What Jesus is by nature (Son of God), we become by grace (sons and daughters of the Father)

C. Resurrection of the body

   1. Death doesn't have the final say (mark of our baptism)

   2. To rise with Christ = raised to a new body

D. Emmaus story

   1. Revealed the Scriptures (Liturgy of the Word)

   2. Breaking of the bread (Liturgy of the Eucharist)

E. Suffering sanctified, turned into a gift of love

F. Ascension; Jesus, the high priest, continually blessing his disciples

V. Conclusion

REVIEW

Following the video presentation (and depending on time), you can review the video with your group or read the workbook responses to the Session Eight discussion questions beginning on page 137.

FOR FURTHER STUDY

The Last Supper and the Passover

There are many points of the Last Supper that connect the Passover meal with Jesus' impending sacrifice for the forgiveness of sins. This is perhaps clearest in the Gospel of Luke, as it makes direct references to the Passover celebrations: "Now the feast of Unleavened Bread drew near, which is called the Passover" (Luke 22:1). "Then came the day of Unleavened Bread, on which the Passover lamb had to be sacrificed" (Luke 22:7). "So Jesus sent Peter and John, saying, 'Go and prepare the Passover for us, that we may eat it'" (Luke 22:8). "They went, and found it as he had told them; and they prepared the Passover" (Luke 22:13). And "I have earnestly desired to eat this Passover with you before I suffer" (Luke 22:15).

The Jewish feast of Passover is structured around four cups of wine. Matthew and Mark mention one cup in their accounts of the Last Supper. Luke mentions two cups of wine. The second one is the cup Jesus consecrates. We know from St. Paul that this is the third cup of the Passover seder, because in 1 Corinthians Paul calls it by the technical name for the third cup, the "cup of blessing": "The cup of blessing which we bless, is it not a participation in the blood of Christ?" (1 Corinthians 10:16). At an ordinary Passover seder, the head of the household would take the bread and identify what it represents. At the Last Supper, Jesus "took bread, and when he had given thanks he broke it and gave it to them, saying, 'This is my body which is given for you'" (Luke 22:19). Jesus furthermore exhorts the disciples, "Do this in remembrance of me" (Luke 22:19)—or do this "as my memorial." The Greek word employed here, *anamnēsis*, is often used to translate the Hebrew memorial sacrifices of the Old Testament (of which the Passover was one). Jesus likewise identifies the cup of wine with his blood, "the new covenant in my blood" (Luke 22:20), and mentions the cup as "poured out for you" (Luke 22:20), which is the language of sacrifice.

What we find is that Jesus is himself the Passover lamb. He will be crucified, and his sacrifice will save us for priestly service to the Lord, much as the first Passover sacrifice saved the firstborn sons of Israel for priestly ministry at the time of the Exodus. The sacrifice of the Cross is thus present, in an unbloody way, in Jesus' sacrificial Passover meal at the Last Supper, where he gives his disciples his Body and Blood under the appearance of bread and wine. Likewise, the Passover sacrifice of the Last Supper in the Upper Room was fulfilled on the Cross.

◆ ❖ ◆

St. Peter and the Papacy

All four of the canonical Gospels (Luke, Matthew, Mark, and John) emphasize the key role of Peter, who is the vicar of Christ and the first pope of the Catholic Church. The Gospel of Mark shows Peter as Christ's representative and the representative of the other apostles throughout. In fact, many scenes in Mark's Gospel are told from Peter's perspective, which fits the tradition that Mark's Gospel is a summation of Peter's preaching in Rome. This would also explain why Mark begins with the baptism of John the Baptist, precisely where Peter's preaching begins (as recorded in Luke's Acts of the Apostles). Acts' depiction of Peter's preaching follows the basic outline of Mark's Gospel.

In the Gospel of Matthew, we find Peter listed as "first" (*protos* in Greek) in the list of apostles. In fact, Peter is always listed as first (and Judas the betrayer as last) in all versions of the list of the apostles, even when those lists differ from each other in other ways. In Matthew's account, however, "first" is an adjective—modifying Peter as "the first," or the one with "primacy," of "prime importance"—rather than simply an adverb, as if it were pointing out his place within the list (see Matthew 10:2).

In response to Jesus' question "Who do you say that I am?" (Luke 9:20), Luke's Gospel details Peter's confession that Jesus is the Christ of God. The most complete account of this moment is found in Matthew's Gospel. In Matthew 16, Jesus does several things. He gives Simon the new name "Peter" (from the Greek for "rock"); he declares that he will build his Church upon Peter as the rock; and he gives to Peter, and Peter alone, the keys of the kingdom of heaven, along with the ability to bind and loose. All twelve apostles later receive the ability to bind and loose (Matthew 18), but Peter alone wields the keys (Matthew 16:19).

In Luke's Gospel, during the Last Supper, Jesus highlights in part the purpose of Peter's position of authority. After declaring that Satan will sift all the apostles like wheat, Jesus tells Peter, "But I have prayed for you that your faith may not fail; and when you have turned again, strengthen your brethren" (Luke 22:32). He thus describes Peter's position as one of a servant-leader who acts for the sake of others' faith and strength.

In John's Gospel, after the Resurrection, Jesus reinstates Peter as the shepherd of his flock (John 21). Throughout the Old Testament, God is depicted as the shepherd of Israel; in John's Gospel, Jesus is identified as the Good Shepherd. Following the Resurrection, Jesus appears to Peter and instructs him to "feed my lambs" (John 21:15), "tend my sheep" (John 21:16), and "feed my sheep" (John 21:17). Jesus is clearly giving Peter his orders, making him the shepherd of God's People in his place—a role which Peter officially takes up in the first part of Acts.

♦ ❖ ♦

The Road to Emmaus

After his Resurrection, Jesus meets two disciples on the road to Emmaus. As he walks with them, he takes them through the Old Testament (the Law, the Psalms, and the Prophets), showing how the Scriptures speak about him. Later, he breaks bread with them—and when they finally recognize him, he disappears from their sight.

This is basically how the Eucharistic Liturgy unfolds. First, we have the readings from Scripture and a homily explaining how the Old and New Testaments relate, how Christ is hidden in the Old and how the New makes the Old Testament prefiguration of Christ manifest. Then follows the Eucharist, the "breaking of the bread," where Christ, though hidden from sight, is in plain view.

Notice that during the events at Emmaus, Luke uses the same or similar phrases to describe what happens at the Last Supper and at the table in Emmaus, emphasizing the Eucharistic theme: Jesus "took the bread," "broke it, and" gave "thanks" or "blessed" it, "broke it and gave it to them" (Luke 22:19; Luke 24:30). Jesus is no longer present, as it were, but they recognize him in the breaking of the bread (Luke 24:35).

Luke names one of the disciples on the road to Emmaus as Cleopas. The unnamed disciple is sometimes identified in the Eastern Christian tradition as the Luke himself. If this is the case, we might be able to understand the Gospel of Luke as a reflection of Jesus' discussion with these two disciples, showing how the Old Testament pointed to him. Luke's Gospel thus could be understood as an extended walk with Jesus, highlighting the ways he fulfills the Old Testament in his life, teaching, death, and Resurrection, all within a liturgical context that puts us in touch with the risen Lord himself.

The Journey to Emmaus by Siegfried Detler Bendixen

SESSION

Answers

RESPONSES TO THE DISCUSSION QUESTIONS

Study participants: We encourage you to review the responses for each session after your small group has met and before you begin preparing for the next session.

Study facilitators: In the responses on the following pages, the author provides information and guidance that will help you draw out the varied insights of your group during the discussions. As you prepare for each session, we suggest that you complete the readings and answer the questions on your own before you read the responses.

SESSION ONE

Answers

Session One: Introduction

When we read the Gospels, we hope to learn more about Jesus, the one whom we should love above all others. In what ways has Jesus touched your life?

Answers will vary. Reflecting on how Jesus has touched your life in a personal way can help remind you of why you hope to know more about Jesus through this Bible study.

What do you already know about the Gospel of Luke? What do you hope to learn from your study of Luke's Gospel?

Answers will vary. Discussion on this point may help set expectations for the study. The more you already know about the Gospel of Luke, the more you will benefit from further study. It might be helpful to jot down what you would like to gain from this study so that you can later evaluate how fruitful it was.

SESSION TWO

Answers

Session Two: Luke 1–3

Day 2

Luke 1 presents a parallel contrast between Zechariah and Mary. The angel Gabriel appears to both, with a similar message for each of them. How does Zechariah's reaction to Gabriel's news compare with Mary's? What is the essential difference between their responses? What are the results of their individual responses?

In response to the angel Gabriel's news, both Zechariah and Mary ask how—but there is a subtle difference between them. When Gabriel announces the birth of John the Baptist, Zechariah's response is doubt: "How shall I know this? For I am an old man, and my wife is advanced in years" (Luke 1:18). Zechariah knew God had worked similar miracles in the past, as with Abraham and Sarah (see Genesis 21), yet he does not believe the angel's message. Because he does not believe, he is unable to speak until after John is born (see Luke 1:20). In contrast, when Gabriel announces God's message to Mary, she inquires, "How can this be, since I have no husband?" (Luke 1:34). The difference here is that Mary believes the angel's message; her question is specifically about how she will maintain her virginity, which she intends to retain even after marriage. Her question is not one of disbelief but of faithful trust. As a result, Gabriel reassures her that "with God nothing will be impossible" (Luke 1:37).

Day 3

Old Testament Connection: The first chapter of 1 Samuel begins with a barren woman, Hannah, praying for a son. The Lord hears her prayer, and Hannah bears Samuel, who will become a great prophet and the last judge of Israel. Read Hannah's prayer in 1 Samuel 2:1–10, and then reread Mary's words in Luke 1:46–55. How are these prayers similar?

Mary's prayer in Luke 1:46–55 expresses her profound humility and joy at the miraculous conception of her beloved child. Hannah's prayer is likewise an expression of her deep humility and joy at the conception of her long-awaited child, since she had remained childless for so long. Although her son turns out to be the prophet Samuel, there are many parts of her prayer that point forward to Jesus. In Hebrew Jesus' name means "the Lord's salvation," which Hannah mentions in 1 Samuel 2:1. The very end of Hannah's prayer looks forward to the "anointed" of God (1 Samuel 2:10), which in Hebrew is the Messiah (and in Greek is the Christ).

Day 4

Luke 2:6–12 depicts Jesus being born in utter poverty. When God chose to come among us, in his tremendous providence he chose to be destitute. Why do you think God's Son chose to be born in such poverty?

God chose poverty because he knew we could all relate to such poverty. Some might be able to relate in a very tangible way to physical poverty or financial concerns. Others might recognize the ways in which we have other limits or constraints, such as physical or emotional suffering, an illness, or a spiritual struggle. Since none of us are all-powerful, we will find ourselves "poor" in some regard. The one who is all-powerful chose to relinquish that power to meet us in our need.

Day 5

Luke 2:41–52 describes how Mary and Joseph lost Jesus for three days after they came to Jerusalem for the feast of Passover. This story is included in the Rosary as the fifth Joyful Mystery. What are some ways in which we can lose Jesus for a time? How can we increase our joy at finding him again?

Answers will vary. Some may have lost Jesus by straying from the Faith in their youth and then returning later in life. Others might lose Jesus through mortal sin and return through the Sacrament of Reconciliation. Most of us lose Jesus in small ways through ordinary venial sins and sins of frailty; he still resides in our souls in grace, but our little sins obscure his presence. All of us can lose sight of Jesus because of the distractions of ordinary life. We can probably all grow in joy at remembering Jesus, at finding him anew. We should pray to God to help us increase our joy, just as Mary and Joseph's joy grew upon finding Jesus again in the Temple.

Day 6

Old Testament Connection: Jeremiah and Ezekiel were prophets before and during the time of the Babylonian Exile. Both called God's People to repentance; they also spoke of a new covenant that God would make with his people. Compare the introductions of Jeremiah and Ezekiel (Jeremiah 1:1–3; Ezekiel 1:1–3) with that of John the Baptist (Luke 3:1–6). What are some similarities between these Scripture passages? Why are such details helpful? Why do you think Luke introduces John the Baptist in this way?

All three passages identify the very specific times, places, and rulers during which these prophets heard and proclaimed God's Word. Not only does this give Luke's account of John the Baptist historical credibility; it also echoes the previous prophets. While Jeremiah and Ezekiel announced God's covenant yet to come, John the Baptist proclaimed "the salvation of God" (Luke 3:6) and the arrival of the New Covenant with the coming of Jesus, the Messiah.

Day 7

Reread Luke 3:21–22. Who is present during Jesus' baptism? Who (or what) is specifically mentioned? What can we learn about the nature of God from this moment in Luke's Gospel?

Aside from the people who came to be baptized, these verses mention God the Father, God the Son, and God the Holy Spirit. We see the Father, "a voice ... from heaven," send "the Holy Spirit ... upon" Jesus, declaring Jesus to be his "beloved Son" (Luke 3:22). We can therefore learn from this scene that the one God is a Trinity of Persons; all three members of the Trinity are identified and present in this moment. Likewise, we know that in imitating Jesus by receiving the Sacrament of Baptism, we can become by grace what Jesus is by nature—namely, children of God. (See also CCC 535, 536, 608.)

Session Three: Luke 4–6

Day 9

Old Testament Connection: The prophecy recorded in Isaiah 61 refers to "the year of the Lord's favor" ("the acceptable year of the Lord" in Luke 4:19). This is the Sabbath year (Year of Jubilee), during which slaves were to be released and the land would rest and be restored. Read Isaiah 61. How does this passage relate to the scene in Luke 4:14–30? What is significant about Jesus' teaching, and how do his listeners respond?

Luke 4:14–30 quotes only the first two verses of Isaiah 61, which Jesus declares "has been fulfilled in your hearing." The remainder of Isaiah 61 points ahead to the second coming of Christ at the end of time and the unfolding of his kingdom on earth. (Thus we hear throughout, but especially in the last verse of Isaiah 61, that "the Lord God will cause righteousness and praise to spring forth before all the nations.") By referencing the Old Testament examples of Elijah with the woman of Sidon and Elisha with Naaman the Syrian, Jesus implies that God's invitation of salvation will be extended to the Gentiles, which is what ultimately angers his listeners. (See also CCC 436, 544, 714, 1168, 1286.)

Day 10

Why does Jesus so frequently go to deserted places, as he does in Luke 4:42? What significance does this hold for our personal prayer lives?

Throughout the Gospels, Jesus frequently goes off on his own to deserted places, as we see in Luke 4:42. This is because he is praying to his Father in heaven. Jesus sets us a model here. We, too, need to cultivate silence, at least interior silence, to better focus on and listen to our heavenly Father in prayer.

Day 11

In Jesus' day, it was customary to fish at night on the Lake of Gennesaret. In Luke 5:1–11, we find that Simon Peter and his companions have fished all night without success. Jesus tells them to try one more time; in obeying him, they catch a multitude of fish. Why does this lead Simon Peter to exclaim, "Depart from me, for I am a sinful man, O Lord" (Luke 5:8)?

Simon Peter and his companions were skilled fishermen, and so they would recognize how the multitude of fish was a greater miracle than we might realize at first glance. After working their trade as usual all night and coming up with nothing, Jesus tells them to cast out again—and the catch is massive. But it's not just the large quantity of fish that indicates a miracle; it's also the successful catch at the wrong time of day. All Simon Peter and his companions had to do was obey Jesus' command. This is what allows Simon Peter to recognize that Jesus has worked a miracle and must thus be "Lord."

Day 12

Skeptics sometimes claim that Jesus never said, "I am God." Yet not only are there are many places where he affirms his divine identity when asked (as in Mark 14:61–62); he also says and does things that make it clear he is claiming to be God. Reread Luke 5:20–26. How do Jesus' words and actions here demonstrate his claim to be God?

Jesus clearly claims to have the authority to say that others' sins are forgiven (Luke 5:20, 24). The Pharisees, observing this, clearly recognize the implicit divine claim in his actions when they ask, "Who can forgive sins but God only?" (Luke 5:21). Jesus proceeds to back up his claim to be God by healing the crippled man; the Pharisees can't see whether the man's sins are actually forgiven, but they can see that Jesus has the ability to physically heal the man (Luke 5:23–25).

Day 14

Across the Gospels: Compare Matthew 5:1–12 and Luke 6:20–26. What are some of the differences between these accounts?

Matthew's Beatitudes (5:1–12), which begin his Sermon on the Mount, and Luke's Beatitudes and Woes (6:17–26), which begin his Sermon on the Plain, share much their language and meaning. Among the differences, there are the nine blessings (beatitudes) in Matthew's account compared with the four blessings (beatitudes) in Luke's. There is also the fact that, unlike Matthew, Luke includes woes with warnings of judgment. (See also CCC 2444, 2546–2547.)

Day 14

Carefully read Luke 6:27–36. If we are called to imitate God, what does Jesus' command here tell us about God?

The command to love enemies is one of the most difficult teachings Jesus gives his disciples. It is rooted in God's love, who loved us even when we were his enemies and estranged from him (Romans 5:10).

Session Four: Luke 7–9

Day 16

How does the centurion's response to Jesus (Luke 7:1–10) underscore his great faith? How can you apply this lesson in your life?

The centurion's response is well known and worthy of reflection: "Lord, do not trouble yourself, for I am not worthy to have you come under my roof. ... But say the word, and let my servant be healed" (Luke 7:6–7). With these words, the centurion demonstrates not only his humility but also the strength of his faith. He says he knows Jesus does not even need to be present to answer his request; he believes Jesus has the power to work miracles wherever he is. We can apply this lesson to our faith lives in different ways, and answers will vary. One way is to consider the requests we make to Jesus and try to trust that, if Jesus wills it, no matter how difficult or insurmountable the challenges seem to be, he is all-powerful and can remove the obstacles.

Day 17

In Luke 7:18–23, we read about how John the Baptist sent two of his followers to Jesus, asking if he really was the one "who is to come" or if they should "look for another" (Luke 7:19). What are we to make of Jesus' response?

This is a natural question from John the Baptist since, as we read previously in Session Two, John is suffering in Herod's prison (Luke 3:20). Jesus' response is to remind John the Baptist, and anyone who might have doubts, of what they should expect of the Messiah—and how Jesus has fulfilled the expectations of the Messiah, which they have witnessed.

Day 18

1. Women were somewhat ostracized in antiquity. They were even barred from serving as witnesses in many ancient courtrooms. With that in mind, what does Luke 8:1–3 tell us about Jesus and his relationship with women?

The opening verses of Luke 8 tell us that many women, including those he healed, followed Jesus. These female followers participated in their own way in his ministry. They did not serve in the same way as the male apostles, but they were treated as disciples. This points to the dignity of women and their important place in the early Christian community.

2. What conclusions can be drawn from Luke's account of Jesus' calming the storm on the sea (Luke 8:22–25)?

We can arrive at the same conclusions as the apostles. We too can be reminded that Jesus is none other than the Lord of heaven and earth; all things are under his control. This can give us further confidence that no matter what storms we may encounter in our lives, Jesus is in control. That should give us tremendous comfort.

Day 19

Notice the reaction of many people after Jesus heals the Gerasene demoniac (Luke 8:26–39). The pig herders and those living in the region ask Jesus to depart from them and go somewhere else. This might strike us as odd at first, but their reaction makes sense from a human perspective. All those pigs—their livelihood—were destroyed. In what ways might we react in a similar way to Jesus?

Answers to this question will be very personal. Instead of sharing them publicly, you may want to jot them down and take them to prayer. It might be of interest to note that Jews consider pigs unclean animals, indicating that these pig herders were Gentiles or unfaithful Jews.

We all have areas in our lives—some big, some small—where we are not yet ready to let Jesus take action. As you think of them and write your responses, ask the Lord to help you.

Day 20

1. *Old Testament Connection:* Read 1 Kings 17:8–24. What similarities do you notice between Jesus and Elijah?

In 1 Kings 17:8–24, Elijah miraculously multiplies flour and oil so that he, a widow, and her son will have enough bread for many days. This is similar to Jesus' multiplication of the loaves to feed the crowds. Elijah also raises the widow's son from the dead, just as Jesus raises the son of the widow from Nain from the dead.

2. In Luke 9:10–17, we read how Jesus works a miracle by feeding more than five thousand people with a few loaves of bread. How does this relate to the mystery of the Eucharist?

At the Last Supper, when Jesus institutes the Eucharist, he takes, blesses, and breaks the bread, just as he does when he miraculously multiplies the loaves. Just as the few loaves were multiplied so that all could be fed, in the Eucharist Jesus multiplies himself so that all can be fed by his Body. Finally, just as the miracle of the multiplication of the bread physically nourishes those listening to his teachings, the Eucharist spiritually nourishes Jesus' followers today.

Day 21

It is very difficult to follow Jesus. In Luke 9:57–62, Jesus meets several would-be followers who are caught between their desire to follow Jesus and earthly matters. How do their dilemmas relate to concerns you face in your own life, and how is Jesus calling you to surrender these concerns to him? Also, earlier in Luke, Jesus explains that any who wish to follow him must take up their crosses daily (Luke 9:23). What crosses can you voluntarily take up as part of your Christian life?

Answers will vary. Each of us faces different challenges, responsibilities, and struggles, and how we entrust those cares to God will be different for each person and situation. We have innumerable opportunities to voluntarily deny ourselves in small ways, like fasting, which we can use as mortifications offered up for others. Some ideas: limiting our internet use, going to bed or waking up at a fixed time each day, eating a little more of something we don't especially like at mealtime or a little less of something we really enjoy, listening patiently to someone who annoys us, and smiling at those around us when we do not feel like it.

Session Five: Luke 10-12

Day 23

Jesus often prays to God the Father, and in this chapter of Luke, we see Jesus thanking God the Father. In what ways can we adopt a posture of gratitude when conversing with our heavenly Father? Why is giving thanks an essential attitude for prayer?

Answers will vary. For some, it might be helpful to create a "litany of thanksgiving," listing in prayer the many things they are thankful for. For others, it might be helpful to set a reminder on their phone or an alarm on their watch each hour to pause and thank God for one specific thing. For families, it could be a helpful practice to take turns thanking God for something that happened that day, either at the dinner table or before bedtime. There are many other ways for us to approach God in gratitude. Giving thanks to God is an act of justice, returning to God the honor we owe him. Giving thanks also reminds us of God's goodness and encourages us to share the blessings we have freely received with others.

Day 24

Old Testament Connection: After the old kingdom of Israel split in two, conflicts between the rebellious northern tribes dwelling in Samaria (Israel) and the southern tribes near Jerusalem (Judah) went on for generations. Each saw the other as enemies. During the reign of King Ahaz of Judah, Israel took captive two hundred thousand men from Judah. Read about this conflict and its interesting outcome in 2 Chronicles 28:8–15. What connections can you find between this passage and Jesus' parable of the Good Samaritan (Luke 10:29–37)?

There are various similarities between these two passages. The captives are returned to kinsmen in Jericho; in Jesus' parable, the man is on his way to Jericho. Those who aid the captives are from Samaria; in the parable, the person who helps the man in need is a Samaritan. The captives are clothed, fed, anointed with oil, and placed on donkeys for transport; in the parable, the Samaritan bandages the wounded man, anoints his wounds with oil, and sets him on his donkey to take him to an inn. Both the captives and the wounded man are cared for by those who would otherwise be considered enemies. (See also CCC 1825, 2196, 2822.)

Day 15

Across the Gospels: Read Matthew 6:9–13; then reread Luke 11:2–4. What are the differences between the Lord's Prayer in Matthew and the Lord's Prayer in Luke? In what ways are they similar?

The Lord's Prayer in Matthew is very similar to that in Luke, with only a few differences standing out. First, Luke's version is shorter than Matthew's. In Luke, when we find the petition for forgiveness, it reads, "forgive us our sins" (Luke 11:4), whereas in Matthew the sins are recognized as "trespasses" (Matthew 6:12). Furthermore, the petition to "lead us not into temptation" (Luke 11:4) is where Luke's version ends, whereas Matthew's includes the final line, "but deliver us from evil" (Matthew 6:13).

Day 26

Jesus is often harsher when dealing with the Pharisees and scholars of the law than he is with the ordinary sinners who come to him. What might account for this?

The Pharisees and scholars of the law are the religious teachers and leaders of the people, and yet they, who should know better, are leading the people astray. The biggest criticism Jesus levels against them is their hypocrisy and pride. The sinners who come to Jesus know they need a savior. The Pharisees and scholars of the law, who regularly attempt to trap Jesus, do not seem to recognize their own need for salvation.

Day 27

Consider Jesus' words: "Where your treasure is, there will your heart be also" (Luke 12:34). Where is your heart? In other words, what do you treasure above all else? What are some ways you can turn away from the "treasures" of the world and align your heart with the treasure of God's kingdom?

This is a personal question, and answers will vary. We can ask for the Holy Spirit to reveal to us in prayer what occupies our heart: God or something other than God. We should consider what we are passionate about, what we find ourselves thinking or dreaming about. The things we make sacrifices for or inconvenience ourselves for tend to be a good measure of what matters to us most. It might be people in our lives, money, pleasure, power, success, food, hobbies, specific pursuits and pastimes, and more. Being honest with ourselves and what our main treasures are is the first step in reorienting our hearts toward God and his kingdom. We can also follow Jesus' example and keep our hearts set on God through daily prayer. When our lives are rooted in prayer and in our relationship with God, the rest follows.

Day 28

What makes Jesus a source of "division" (Luke 12:49–53)? What does this tell us about the cost of discipleship?

Jesus is a source of division because he requires us to give him our all, our entire self. When families, work, friends, or anything else comes in the way of Jesus, we still have to put Jesus first. That can create division between ourselves and others, even those who are close to us. The cost of discipleship is that we must die to self and live for God, despite the divisions that this may create close to home. We have to strive to give 100 percent.

Session Six: Luke 13–17

Day 30

In an earlier chapter of Luke's Gospel, Jesus teaches a parable about trees and fruit: "For no good tree bears bad fruit, nor again does a bad tree bear good fruit; for each tree is known by its own fruit" (Luke 6:43–44). In the parable of the barren fig tree, Jesus tells the fate of a tree that bears no fruit (Luke 13:6–9). How are these teachings related?

If the trees represent people, the fruit represents their works: a good person produces good works, whereas an evil person creates bad ones. In this parable, the barren fig tree does not produce any fruit despite the careful tending of the vinedresser, and so the tree's owner wants to cut it down. The significance we can see here is that the barren fig tree represents those who do not produce anything despite the resources and opportunities they have received from God and the expectation that they should do something good with it. The consequence is that, if they do not give God back something good in return for what they have received, they will be cut down (Luke 13:9)—that is, cut off from God's kingdom.

Day 31

What does the parable of the leaven (Luke 13:20–21) tell us about the Kingdom of God?

The parable of the leaven tells us that the Kingdom of God acts like leaven in the world. Just as leaven passes unnoticed in the dough but helps the dough rise, so, too, the faithful members of the Kingdom of God mostly pass unnoticed in the world while adding the "leaven" of Christ, thereby sanctifying the world from within.

Day 32

Across the Gospels: Read Matthew 5:13; then reread Luke 14:34–35. Why does Jesus bring up the importance of salt retaining its taste? How is this a metaphor for the Christian life?

As far as the practical properties of salt are concerned, salt preserves food from corruption and also draws out its underlying flavors. If too little salt is used during the preparation of food, it can affect the flavor of an entire dish. Other than its culinary uses, salt has historically been used to treat injuries: it draws out moisture from wounds, along with contaminants.

In Matthew 5:13, Jesus specifically tells his listeners that they are "the salt of the earth." By this he means his followers should exhibit these same properties: preserving the world from corruption, healing the wounds of sin, and drawing out the inherent goodness of others through virtue and humility. If salt loses its taste, as Jesus mentions in both Matthew's and Luke's Gospels, it is of no use to anyone. In the same way, Christians need to retain their "flavor" (metaphorically) as Christians, or else no one benefits. (It may be interesting to note that salt was an important element in sacrifices and worship in the Old Testament; see Exodus 30:35, Leviticus 2:13, and Ezekiel 43:24.)

Day 33

What does the parable of the lost sheep (Luke 15:1–7) tell us about God?

The parable of the lost sheep communicates God's intense love for us. The shepherd leaves the ninety-nine sheep behind, risking everything for the sake of the one who is lost. In the same way, God relentlessly pursues us, giving up everything to save us. He would be willing to make such a sacrifice for just one of us, as if we were the only concern of his fatherly heart.

Day 34

In the parable of the dishonest steward (Luke 16:1–13), the master commends the dishonest steward for how he acted. What point is Jesus trying to make here? How should we interpret his advice to "make friends for yourselves by means of unrighteous mammon" (Luke 16:9)? How does this relate to his following words: "He who is faithful in a very little is faithful also in much" (Luke 16:10) and "You cannot serve God and mammon" (Luke 16:13)?

It makes sense to clarify that in the parable of the dishonest steward, Jesus is not praising dishonesty but rather is praising the steward's shrewdness. In a way, the master in the parable is saying, "My steward made poor choices and put himself in a bad situation—but you have to give him credit for considering his future options and making it work for himself." With this example, Jesus invites his followers to be honest stewards instead, ones who are faithful in small matters as well as large ones (Luke 16:10). By advising them to "make friends for yourselves by means of unrighteous mammon" (worldly wealth), Jesus encourages his followers to be shrewd in how they conduct themselves in the world. After all, as Jesus tells us, we can either live in and serve this world (mammon) or live in a way that prepares us for the next one world (with God). We cannot spend our lives serving "mammon" and expect to accomplish what God has entrusted to us. But if we can shrewdly and honestly manage our "unrighteous mammon" for the sake of saving up treasures in heaven (Luke 12:33), we will end up receiving those "true riches" (Luke 16:11). (See also CCC 2424.)

Day 35

Old Testament Connection: After the death of King Solomon, ten tribes of Israel rebelled and broke away, dividing the kingdom in two: the Northern Kingdom in Samaria (known as Israel) and the Southern Kingdom near Jerusalem (known as Judah). The Samaritans of Jesus' day were the remnant of the breakaway group and dwelled separately from the Jews. With this context in mind, reread Luke 17:11–19. What is so significant about this scene? Specifically, why ten, and why does Luke emphasize the detail about the Samaritan who returned?

In the case of the lepers who are cleansed by Jesus, only the Samaritan, "the foreigner" (Luke 16:18), came back to thank Jesus. Luke highlights this detail to convey how Jesus is beginning to reunite the People of God who were divided. This echoes the words of the prophet Jeremiah, who prophesied to the rebellious tribes of Israel: "Then I [the Lord] will gather the remnant of my flock out of all the countries where I have driven them, and I will bring them back to their fold" (Jeremiah 23:3). This movement will continue to be fulfilled even more so in Luke's sequel, the Acts of the Apostles, as the Gospel spreads among the Samaritans.

SESSION SEVEN

Answers

Session Seven: Luke 18–21

Day 37

In what ways does the parable of the widow and the unrighteous judge (Luke 18:1–8) reflect our relationship with God? What are the crucial differences between the judge and God?

In the parable, the widow shows us the perseverance in prayer we need in our own relationship with God. Like the widow, we need to be confident and persistent in bringing our needs to God. The crucial difference between the judge and God is that the judge has no concern for the widow except to make her stop pestering him. But God is concerned for us like a loving father, and he listens to us and responds to our prayers out of the love he has for each of us.

Day 38

What can we learn from Zacchaeus, a tax collector who clearly cheated people, and his conversion upon encountering Jesus (Luke 19:1–10)?

Luke gives us three specific details about Zacchaeus straight away: he is a chief tax collector, he is rich, and he is small in stature (Luke 19:2–3). In some ways, all three of these characteristics make it unlikely that Zacchaeus could readily approach Jesus—the first two being moral and social obstacles, and the third a physical obstacle, since he is shorter than most people in the crowds. Still, though he is a sinner, Zacchaeus takes initiative: he climbs a tree to get a better glimpse of Jesus. Then, after welcoming Jesus into his home, Zacchaeus undergoes a conversion. It is curious to observe that, in the RSV-2CE translation of the Bible, Zacchaeus says, "Behold, Lord, the half of my goods I give to the poor; and if I have defrauded any one of anything, I restore it fourfold" (Luke 19:8) He doesn't say "I will give to the poor" or "I promise to restore it"; he says it as if he is already in the act of making atonement for his past sins. We must follow Zacchaeus' example: we must be willing to take initiative in our spiritual lives—and our love for God needs to be backed up by our actions, not solely our sentiments of goodwill. (See also CCC 549, 588, 1443, 2712.)

Day 39

Old Testament Connection: As King David neared the end of his life, he took certain steps to confirm the path of succession for his son Solomon. Read 1 Kings 1:32–40; then reread Luke 19:33–40. What similarities do you notice between these two scenes? How is this moment yet another confirmation of Jesus' identity?

Solomon, riding his father's mule, approaches the river Gihon (near Jerusalem) to be anointed king, the son of David. Jesus likewise rides a mule into Jerusalem and is heralded as the true king, the Messiah, the Son of David.

Day 40

How does the parable of the wicked tenants (Luke 20:9–19) relate to Jesus' conflicts with the religious leaders of Israel?

In the parable of the wicked tenants, the vineyard represents God's People, Israel; the landowner is God himself; and the tenants are the leaders of the people. The messengers whom the tenants reject are God's prophets; the son they kill is Jesus. Jesus is delivering a message that he hopes they recognize as a sign of judgment. (See also CCC 587.)

Day 41

Religious Context: In Jesus' day, the Sadducees were a Jewish sect that represented the priestly aristocracy. Unlike the Pharisees, the Sadducees believed that only the first five books of Moses (the Torah) were God's divinely inspired Word. They did not accept doctrines such as the resurrection of the dead or the existence of angels.

Reread Luke 20:27–40. How are the Sadducees, who don't believe in the resurrection, trying to trap Jesus? How does Jesus effectively dismantle their trap?

With their question about the wife with seven husbands, the Sadducees are trying to show how foolish the idea of resurrection is. They think that if resurrection exists, you could have a woman with multiple husbands. Jesus first explains to them that at the resurrection, people will "neither marry" nor be "given in marriage" (Luke 20:35). Then, to support resurrection itself, Jesus refers to the Scriptures that the Sadducees acknowledge as God's Word. Jesus uses the famous passage from Exodus 3, when God appeared to Moses in the burning bush, to support how God is "not God of the dead, but of the living; for all live to him" (Luke 20:38). (See also CCC 575.)

Day 42

How can we apply Jesus' point about the widow's offering (Luke 21:1–4) to our own lives?

Answers will vary. Jesus points out that the size of the offering we make isn't as important as the love with which we give it. We should recognize that all that we have received is from God and, by rights, should be given back to God. We should make a return to the Lord out of love, giving him all that we have and placing our confidence in him. (See also CCC 2544.)

Session Eight: Luke 22-24

Day 44

Old Testament Connection: Exodus 24 recounts how God established a covenant with Israel through Moses while they were at Mount Sinai. The covenant was sealed with a sacrifice. Read about this event in Exodus 24:5-11; then reread Luke 22:19-20. What similarities do you notice between these two passages?

In Exodus, Moses throws the blood of the sacrifice upon the people and says, "Behold the blood of the covenant" (Exodus 24:8); Jesus likewise takes the cup filled with wine at the Last Supper and calls it the blood of the "new covenant" (Luke 22:20), offering himself as the sacrifice that ratifies it. In Exodus, the people eat and drink in the presence of God; in a similar way, the disciples at the Last Supper eat and drink the Passover meal in the presence of the Son of God.

Day 45

Old Testament Connection: Daniel lived during the Babylonian Exile, serving in the court of the Babylonian king Nebuchadnezzar. Daniel received many prophetic and apocalyptic visions. Read the imagery of one such vision in Daniel 7:13-14; then reread the scene about Jesus before the chief priests and scribes in Luke 22:66-70. How do you interpret Jesus' comments to the council? How do they parallel Daniel 7?

In Daniel 7, the prophet Daniel has a vision of "one like a son of man" coming on "the clouds of heaven," who was presented before "the Ancient of Days" (Daniel 7:13). This "son of man" figure is "given dominion" over the whole world (Daniel 7:14). In his remarks to the council, Jesus clearly refers to this passage and identifies himself as the messianic figure.

Day 46

Historical Context: Herod Antipas, son of Herod the Great, was the tetrarch who ruled over the region of Galilee at the time of Jesus. Herod's family was not ethnically Jewish; he descended from the Idumean converts to Judaism during the time of the Maccabean revolt. Reread Luke 23:6–9. With this context in mind, what is the irony behind Jesus' confrontation with Herod?

The Herodians were "mock kings" over Israel. Herod Antipas, who confronts Jesus, was a son of Herod the Great, a client king for Rome. (Herod Antipas retained control of Galilee after Herod the Great's "kingdom" was divided.) While the Herodian claim to rule was grounded in false messianic interpretations and political aspirations, Jesus, as the true heir to the throne of King David, had a legitimate claim to rule. In contrast to his confrontations with the high priest and with Pilate, Jesus doesn't speak at all to Herod.

Day 47

Across the Gospels: There are three "last sayings" of Jesus in Luke's Gospel (Luke 23:34, 43, 46). These three last sayings are not found in the other Gospels. What do these words spoken by Jesus from the Cross tell us about him?

Jesus' prayer to the Father to forgive the sins of his adversaries shows his mercy. While Jesus was on the Cross, his comment to the thief—that soon he will be with Jesus in Paradise—shows Jesus' love. Finally, by committing his spirit into the Father's hands, Jesus shows his trust in the Father and his desire to return to heaven.

Day 48

How does the story of the disciples on the road to Emmaus (Luke 24:13–35) mirror what happens during the Catholic Mass?

Both the walk to Emmaus and the Sacred Liturgy begin with the opening of the Scriptures; in the Mass, we read the Old Testament in the forward-pointing context of Christ in the New Testament. The readings are followed by "the breaking of the bread" (Luke 24:35), where Jesus is recognized in the Eucharist. Finally, both end with a type of "sending": in the same way the disciples return to proclaim Jesus' Resurrection, we are sent forth from Mass to proclaiming the Good News to the world. (See also CCC 1346–1347.)

Day 49

Why might Jesus' ascension (Luke 24:50–51) be considered both a joyous and a sorrowful event?

Answers will vary. It might be a sorrowful event in that Jesus' physical departure from the disciples is the end of that phase of their relationship with him. No longer will he walk among them as he had before. From heaven, however, Jesus sends us the gift of the Holy Spirit (CCC 667). It is thus joyful in that now the Holy Spirit—the "power from on high" that Jesus promises in Luke 24:49—can descend. Through the Holy Spirit, Jesus can always be made present through the sacraments to everyone around the world, without the physical limitations he previously had with his earliest disciples. Another reason this is a joyful moment is that now Christ intercedes for us and continually blesses us from heaven (CCC 662). In fact, in the very passage from Luke's Gospel (Luke 24:50–51), we see Jesus blessing his apostles as he ascends. This is what he does as high priest in heaven (see Hebrews 2:17, 4:14–15, and 8:1). We must bear in mind that Jesus' ascension is not merely a departure; it glorifies humanity by bringing Jesus' human nature into the heavenly Kingdom of God (CCC 665).

Icons Attributed to St. Luke the Evangelist

Our Lady of Perpetual Help
CHURCH OF ST. ALPHONSUS LIGUORI, ROME

Salus Populi Romani
BASILICA OF ST. MARY MAJOR, ROME

Icons Attributed to St. Luke | 141

Our Lady of Vladimir
CHURCH OF ST. NICHOLAS IN TOLMACHI, MOSCOW

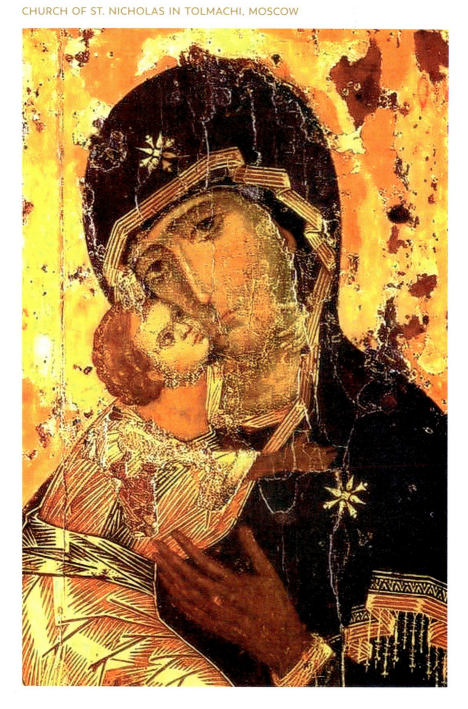

Our Lady of Czestochowa
JASNA GORA MONASTERY, CZESTOCHOWA

Photo credit Robert Drózd

NOTES

1. St. Justin Martyr, one of the early Church Fathers, wrote in his *Apologies,* "And on the day called Sunday there is a meeting in one place of those who live in cities or the country, and the memoirs of the apostles or the writings of the prophets are read as long as time permits. When the reader has finished, the president in a discourse urges and invites [us] to the imitation of these noble things." Justin, *First Apology,* ed. and trans. Edward Rochie Hardy, in *Early Christian Fathers,* ed. Cyril C. Richardson (Philadelphia: Westminster Press, 1953), 67, ccel.org.

2. Origen says on Romans 16:21, "Some maintain that this very Lucius is Luke, who wrote the Gospel, since it is customary for names to be given sometimes in accordance with the native declensions, sometimes even according to the Greek or Roman declension." Origen, *Commentary on the Epistle to the Romans, Books 6–10,* trans. Thomas P. Scheck (Washington, DC: Catholic University of America Press, 2002), 304 (10.39.1–2).

3. Jerome, *On Illustrious Men* [*De Viris Illustribus*], ed. D.P. Curtin, trans. Ernest Cushing Richardson (Philadelphia: Dalcassian, 2017), 10, books.google.com.

4. The current title is *The New Testament Documents: Are They Reliable?,* 6th ed. (Grand Rapids, MI: Eerdmans; Downers Grove, IL: Intervarsity, 1981).

5. Flavius Josephus, *Antiquities of the Jews* 18.1–3.

6. Brant Pitre, *Jesus and the Last Supper* (Grand Rapids, MI: Eerdmans, 2015), 141.

7. *Antiquities of the Jews* 8.2.

FOR FURTHER READING

These are selected author's sources that may be of special interest to study participants:

Bauckham, Richard. *Jesus and the Eyewitnesses: The Gospels as Eyewitness Testimony.* Grand Rapids, MI: Eerdmans, 2006.

Benedict XVI (Joseph Ratzinger). *Jesus of Nazareth*, vol. 1, *From the Baptism in the Jordan to the Transfiguration,* trans Adrian Walker. New York: Doubleday, 2007.

Bruce, F.F. *The New Testament Documents: Are They Reliable?* 6th ed. Grand Rapids, MI: Eerdmans; Downers Grove, IL: InterVarsity, 1981 (1943).

Burridge, Richard A. *What Are the Gospels? A Comparison with Graeco-Roman Biography.* 2nd ed. Grand Rapids, MI: Eerdmans, 2004.

Gadenz, Pablo T. *The Gospel of Luke.* Grand Rapids, MI: Baker Academic, 2018.

Hahn, Scott. *The Fourth Cup: Unveiling the Mystery of the Last Supper and the Cross.* New York: Image, 2018.

Hahn, Scott. *Hail, Holy Queen: The Mother of God in the Word of God.* New York: Doubleday, 2001.

Hahn, Scott W. *Kinship by Covenant: A Canonical Approach to the Fulfillment of God's Saving Promises.* New Haven, CT: Yale University Press, 2009.

Hahn, Scott and Curtis Mitch, eds. *Ignatius Catholic Study Bible: New Testament.* 2nd Catholic ed. San Francisco: Ignatius, 2010.

Pelikan, Jaroslav. *Acts.* Grand Rapids, MI: Brazos, 2005.

Pitre, Brant. *Jesus and the Jewish Roots of Mary: Unveiling the Mother of the Messiah.* New York: Image, 2018.

Pitre, Brant. *Jesus and the Jewish Roots of the Eucharist: Unlocking the Secrets of the Last Supper.* New York: Doubleday, 2011.

Pitre, Brant. *Jesus and the Last Supper.* Grand Rapids, MI: Eerdmans, 2015.

Strelan, Rick. *Luke the Priest: The Authority of the Third Gospel.* Aldershot, UK; Burlington, VT: Ashgate, 2008.

ABOUT THE AUTHORS AND PRESENTERS

Jeff Cavins is recognized nationally and internationally as one of the most effective and engaging speakers in the Church today. After twelve years as a Protestant pastor, Jeff returned to the Catholic Church under the guidance of Bishop Paul Dudley. Over the past several decades, Jeff has dedicated his life to developing *The Bible Timeline: The Story of Salvation,* a practical, interactive program that helps people understand the "big picture" of God's plan of salvation in Sacred Scripture. Jeff was the host of EWTN's *Life on the Rock* for six years and has appeared widely on Catholic radio, television, and digital media. For his contributions to *The Bible in a Year* podcast, Jeff was recognized as one of Our Sunday Visitors' Catholics of the Year for 2021 and was a recipient of the 2022 Cardinal John P. Foley Award for excellence and innovation in Catholic storytelling.

Dr. Jeffrey Morrow is professor of theology at Franciscan University of Steubenville and is the director of the St. Paul Studies Center at the St. Paul Center for Biblical Studies. He is a series editor for the Catholic University of America Press' *Verbum Domini* series. Among his other publications are *Jesus' Resurrection: A Jewish Convert Examines the Evidence*; *Liturgy and Sacrament, Mystagogy and Martyrdom*; *Modern Biblical Criticism as a Tool of Statecraft (1700–1900),* coauthored with Scott Hahn; and *Murmuring Against Moses: The Contentious History and Contested Future of Pentateuchal Studies,* coauthored with John Bergsma. Jeff holds a doctorate and a master's degree in Catholic theology from the University of Dayton.

PROGRAM CREDITS

EXECUTIVE PRODUCER & PUBLISHER
Jonathan Strate

GENERAL MANAGERS
Jeffrey Cole
Dcn. John Harden

PROJECT MANAGER
Veronica Salazar

PRODUCT MANAGER
Elisa Tremblay

LUKE VIDEO SERIES
SENIOR VIDEO PRODUCER
Matthew Pirrall

VIDEO CREATIVE DIRECTOR
Matthew Longua

PRODUCTION MANAGER
Teresa Seale

FEATURING
Jeff Cavins
Dr. Jeffrey Morrow

LUKE WRITTEN MATERIALS
AUTHORS & WRITERS
Jeff Cavins
Dr. Jeffrey Morrow

CONTENT REVIEWERS
Dcn. John Harden
Elisa Tremblay

GRAPHIC DESIGN
Becca Cabell
Sarah Stueve
Stella Ziegler

COVER DESIGN
Sarah Stueve
Faceout Studio

PRINT EDITORIAL
Christina Eberle
Rebecca Robinson

MARKETING
Julia Morgensai
Maria Ruedisueli

NOTES

NOTES